Nigel Brown

The History of the
Manchester Geographical Society
1884-1950

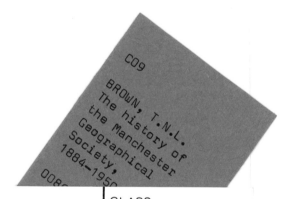

T Nigel L Brown

The History of the
Manchester Geographical
Society

1884–1950

Manchester University Press

00865446

© 1971 Manchester Geographical Society

Published by
Manchester University Press
316–324 Oxford Road
Manchester M13 9NR

ISBN 0 7190 1251 1

Made and printed in Great Britain by
Butler & Tanner Ltd., Frome and London

Contents

Introductory note

It is a great honour to have been asked to introduce this History of the Manchester Geographical Society which was discovered among Mr. T. N. L. Brown's papers after his untimely death. The Council considers that its publication will be a lasting memorial to him and Members have contributed to 'The Nigel Brown Memorial Fund' to help to defray the cost. Professor Brian Rodgers has written an appreciation which reveals the breadth and high quality of Nigel Brown's work for the Society and it only remains for me to emphasize the debt that the Council and members owe to him for his devoted service. Nigel Brown lifted the Society out of its post-war doldrums and inspired groups of Members to work enthusiastically at such projects as the Lymm Survey and the reorganization of the Library. His book shows his scholarly approach to the History but only the members know how much his warm humanity helped to weld the Society into the active, successful and friendly body that it is today. This Society has always been fortunate in its Officers and not least in Nigel Brown who followed and upheld the great traditions of his predecessors.

M. D. Leigh
President 1967–70

Acknowledgement
Mrs. Irene Brown wishes to thank Miss Leigh and other members of Council and of the Society who have helped in bringing about the publication of this history.

Sources
Sources consulted include the *Journal of the Manchester Geographical Society*, its Council Minutes, Executive Committee Minutes, scrap books, General Purposes Minutes, and the Minutes of the Education and Finance Committees.

Foreword

Nigel Brown: An appreciation

Nigel Brown's *History of the Manchester Geographical Society* concludes appropriately with the first mention of his own name; had it continued to cover more recent years, it must inevitably have become a stocktaking of his own immense efforts to strengthen the Society over a period of more than twenty years of tireless and unselfish work. A member since 1947, he became Honorary Editor in 1950, Honorary Secretary in 1952, and was President between 1961 and 1964.

Perhaps his chief ambition was to bring the Society and the University Department into a closer relationship; as a Cambridge graduate in Geography and Anthropology, serving as an Administrative Officer in the Bursar's Department of the university, he was ideally qualified to attempt the difficult task of reconciling amateur and professional interests. He had substantial success; members of the staff of the Department served on Council, and Professor P. R. Crowe was President from 1958 to 1961.

The *Journal* was revived, after a lapse of some years, as an essentially academic publication, but only a single issue was published in this new form before it became a casualty of shortage of funds. As Secretary, Nigel Brown was insistent that a number of professional geographers should appear in each year's programme of speakers, and he did his best to make sure that an attractive and increasingly ambitious range of summer excursions was maintained. Indeed, under his energetic leadership, the 1950's were a period of vigour and progress in the Society: a lecture in the Free Trade Hall by Sir Edmund Hillary on the Conquest of Everest in 1953 recalled its palmiest days; an appeal fund made possible substantial re-decoration and repair of the premises and the re-assembly of the somewhat scattered (but very valuable) collection of early atlases made it possible for a very substantial sum to be raised by their transfer to the university.

Any Society like the Manchester Geographical Society must depend on the hard work and enthusiasm of a small nucleus of its members, and even among these there must be one or two willing horses prepared to pull hardest in the traces. Without them, no voluntary association can survive. Nigel Brown's death at an early age has deprived the Society of a source of great strength, and it will be fortunate indeed if it succeeds in replacing him. Yet his services to the Society that formed so large a part of his life have not ceased with his death, for he has left behind him this history that describes the rise of the pioneer provincial geographical society. What part the growth of a 'lay' interest in geography played in establishing the academic study of the subject in the universities is clearly a large question; but there is no doubt that this case-study contains much that will interest future historians of the development of geography in Britain.

H. B. Rodgers
Professor of Social Geography
University of Keele

I
Background and progenitors to 1884

At a meeting at the Chamber of Commerce in 1879 to discuss the promotion of trade with Africa, the Bishop of Salford (later Cardinal Vaughan) made pointed reference to the activities of numerous commercial geographical societies on the Continent and elsewhere. He drew attention to the dependence of the cotton trade on foreign exports and the need of a knowledge of geography to secure new markets and alternative sources of raw material; the American Civil War had caused great hardship in Lancashire when it stopped imports of raw cotton.

A number of prominent Mancunians, amongst them the Bishop, the President of the Chamber of Commerce, C. P. Scott, Professor Boyd Dawkins, J. F. Hutton, business men and members of Parliament, tried to found a Society of Commercial Geography but the attempt failed.

Though the failure of the Society of Commercial Geography seemed to suggest that Manchester thought itself sufficiently well informed on matters geographical, foreign competition brought a great change for the worse in the commercial world. The discoveries of Livingstone, Speke, Cameron and others brought about the extraordinarily rapid opening up of Africa, whilst the seventy Continental geographical societies were diligent in bringing before their respective governments the prime value of colonial possessions in commerce, and the need to stake early claims. Portugal, for instance, began to see the worth of her West African possessions in a new and astonishing light, and so endeavoured to add control of the Congo to that she already possessed over the Zambesi, and other Continental countries were equally watchful of their own interests. This emergence of a new and commercially rich continent resulted in more attention being paid to geography, particularly in Britain where Manchester, amongst other cities, suddenly awoke to the strong foreign challenge in the commercial and colonial fields and to the prodigious developments in Africa.

The Bishop of Salford, John Slagg and a few friends were still convinced that there was urgent need of a geographical society in

Manchester. The first attempt had failed through apathy, and as the Bishop thought, through being too ambitious, but the pioneers still had great faith, and regarded the earlier venture merely as a reconnaissance. Hearing of the attempt of Commander V. L. Cameron to set up a British Commercial Geographical Society in London, and of other developments in Scotland, they sensed that the time was opportune to raise the matter again. Consequently, a meeting was arranged in the Town Hall on 15 October 1884, with the Lord Mayor (Councillor P. Goldschmidt) as Chairman, at which a new Provisional Committtee was appointed to draw up draft rules, and to make preliminary enquiries concerning accommodation and the publication of a journal. It is interesting to find that the new Provisional Committee included fifteen of those who had worked for the former society, and that for the eighteen who served only on the first committee, forty-four new adherents sat on the new body. Significantly too, the support from the Chamber of Commerce had greatly increased, as had that from local members of Parliament. As Honorary Secretary there was appointed a new convert to the cause, one Eli Sowerbutts, an accountant. Quite how he became associated with the society is not known, but one suspects that it resulted from political activities during the course of which John Slagg found a kindred spirit who had already shown his geographical interests in lectures and talks. At all events, this new appointment proved to be of the greatest importance.

The timing of this meeting had been arranged with some care for J. F. Hutton, still a keen 'geographer', had had the inspiration to arrange a visit to Manchester from H. M. Stanley, then at the peak of his fame. His address was at the Free Trade Hall on 21 October 1884, entitled 'Central Africa and the Congo Basin', bore the subtitle 'The Importance of the Scientific Study of Geography' and contained an impassioned appeal for the establishment of local societies, which raised the enthusiasm of his vast audience to fever pitch and ensured a good reception in the local press.

Encouraged by such excellent publicity from a national hero, the Provisional Committee met on 12 November 1884, setting up a sub-committee to prepare a constitution, and arranging for the issue of 3000 circulars. Working fast, and basing their recommendations largely on the Rules of the Society of Commercial Geography, the sub-committee reported on 3 December, and the draft rules were accepted. Response to the circulars had been encouraging, and so a first meeting of the Society was called on the evening of 27 January 1885 in the Lecture Hall of the Athenaeum. Not as many attended this meeting as some of the enthusiasts had hoped, but quite a respectable audience heard it announced that there had been 320 promises of membership, made up of 2 life, 295 ordinary and 23 associate members. The Chairman (J. F. Hutton, President of the Chamber of Commerce) then delivered the inaugural address, in the course of which he said that

> When we see a continual lack of prosperity in old markets and in old grooves of trade, surely that is a sign of the necessity for the search of new ones; and it is high time to realize what other nations are doing and to exert ourselves to know more of the world and of its resources. Unless we do this, our commerce and industries must decline, and England will be unable to maintain the position she has so long held.

Later he added

> Founding a geographical society means the determination to acquire a knowledge of every country, sea, river and mountain and to study the nature, condition and needs of the peoples of the earth. The encouragement of such study is erecting one of the mainstays of commerce.

From such remarks it appears that the prime appeal of the new society was still directed towards the business men of Lancashire rather than towards the educationalists, and that the anticipated work would be in the commercial field rather than in the scientific aspects.

In proposing the adoption of the Provisional Committee's report, however, Bishop Vaughan of Salford introduced evidence of wider interests, envisaging the society spreading the knowledge of geography as there was such need of something or somebody to enlighten the ignorance of many, even educated, persons on that subject. But far beyond the promotion of science or even the promotion of commerce, was another consideration; to raise, civilize, Christianize the immense majority of the human family who were thought to be living in a state of utter darkness, in the deepest moral degradation, without any knowledge of civilization or of

3

Christianity, and without even a desire to come out of this Slough of Despond.

Jacob Bright expressed the point of view of a member of Parliament, saying that he was not sure that the public men of this country, even members of the House of Commons, were remarkable for their knowledge of geography. But if flourishing geographical societies brought pressure to bear, public men would have to pay much more attention to this important branch of education. He also drew attention to the fact that ladies were to be admitted on the same footing as men. The second Provisional Committee had included just one, Miss Becker, and in March 1885 Mrs. A. H. Wood of Plymouth Grove, and Miss Fanny Rutherford of the Lancashire Independent College, Whalley Range, were formally elected. This simple fact, testifying to the foresight of the founders, was to prove of great wisdom later for Manchester avoided the bitter controversy that split the Royal Geographical Society from top to bottom in the period 1867–1913.

Lord Aberdare, the active President of the Royal Geographical Society, travelled up to Manchester to be present at the inaugural meeting. The London Society, after a good start, followed by a period in the doldrums, was once again forging ahead, considerably helped by the publicity brought to geography by the creation of Section E of the British Association, the new interest in Africa, and more particularly by the sheer ability of presidents such as Murchison and administrators such as Galton and Freshfield. Lord Aberdare himself took a keen interest in the opening up of Africa, being amongst other things, Chairman of the National African Association, the forerunner of the Royal Niger Company.

Aberdare brought the good wishes of the Royal Geographical Society which had been founded fifty-five years earlier, for the promotion and diffusion of geographical knowledge. The last half century had seen a marvellous increase in our knowledge and it could be said, with the strictest regard for truth, that the great proportion of it was due to the Royal Geographical Society which had sent out many expeditions at its own cost and had collected an enormous mass of information. He could not but think that the simultaneous foundation of societies in Manchester and Edinburgh was proof that the country was waking up at last to a sense of the necessity for a diffusion of geographical knowledge. His society had also taken the utmost pains to train geographers. In Germany no less than seven professorships had been endowed for the special teaching of geography, and in France there were also seven professors paid by the State. In spite of a memorial presented to the Universities Commissioners in 1879, there was nothing of this kind in this country. With our enormous colonial empire, occupying one fifth of the globe, we had not taken the necessary means of acquainting ourselves with its situation and products. If we could look into the records of the Foreign and Colonial Offices, we should probably find many an irretrievable blunder made through want of geographical knowledge.

After Professor Boyd Dawkins (Professor of Geology at Owens College), Arthur Arnold, M.P., and Frederick Holmwood (H.M. Consul at Zanzibar) had spoken, the meeting elected Officers and Council for the first year, as follows.

Vice-Presidents: The Rt. Rev. the Lord Bishop of Manchester, Jacob Bright, M.P., Sir J. C. Lee, KT., J.P., The Rt. Rev. the Lord Bishop of Salford, Samuel Ogden, J.P., the Very Rev. Monsignor Gadd, the Rt. Hon. Lord Egerton of Tatton, J. K. Cross, M.P., Oliver Heywood, J.P., The Rt. Hon. Lord Winmarleigh, F. W. Grafton, M.P., H. M. Steinthal, The Vice-Chancellor of Victoria University, W. H. Houldsworth, M.P., The Very Rev. the Dean of Manchester, Henry Lee, M.P., B. Armitage, M.P., John Stagg, M.P., A. Arnold, M.P., The Lord Mayor of Manchester.

Trustees: Alderman C. Makinson, J.P., Councillor P. Goldschmidt, J.P., James Jardine, J.P.

Honorary Secretaries: A. R. Galle, Fritz Zimmern.

Honorary Treasurer: T. R. Wilkinson.

Council: H. M. Steinthal (Chairman), Rev. L. C. Casartelli, M.A., PH.D., W. Mather, J.P., J. F. Hutton (Vice-Chairman), V. K. Armitage, M.A., J.P., Alfred Nield, Professor Sir Henry Roscoe, LL.D., F.R.S., Henry Samson, J.P., Henry Newall, J.P., Professor W. Boyd Dawkins, M.A., F.R.S., E. J. Broadfield, B.A., J. H. Nodal, Professor T. H. Core, M.A., S. Dill, M.A., H. J. Roby, M.A., Professor A. Hopkinson, M.A., B.C.L., Elijah Helm, Mark Stirrup, F.G.S., Professor A. W. Ward, LITT. D., J. Thewlis Jhonson, Rev. Canon Holgate Brown, M.A., George Lord.

This account of the inauguration is interesting for the light it throws on the varying approaches to the new society by different sections of the Manchester population: the purely financial and commercial, the educational and the missionary aspects. It also hints at the deplorable state of geographical teaching in this country at the time. Moreover, the lukewarm support of 1879–80 had been replaced by enthusiasm from some of the most influential men in the district. At the conclusion of the meeting hopes ran high and the new organization prepared to swing into action.

Before going further, however, it is interesting to review the 'Object and Work' in the constitution to enable the reader to appreciate the declared aims and to assess to what degree they were achieved:

The object of the Manchester Geographical Society is to promote the study of all branches of Geographical Science, especially in its relation to commerce and civilization. The work of the Society shall be:—

(1) To further in every way the pursuit of the science as by the study of official and scientific documents, by communications with learned, industrial and commercial societies, by correspondence with consuls, men of science, explorers, missionaries and travellers and by the encouragement of the teaching of geography in schools and colleges.

(2) To hold meetings at which papers shall be read or lectures delivered by members or others.

(3) To examine the possibility of opening new markets to commence and collect information as to the number, character, needs, natural products and resources of such populations as have not yet been brought into relation with British commerce and industry.

(4) To promote and encourage in such way as may be found expedient either alone or in conjunction with other societies, the exploration of the less known regions of the earth.

(5) To enquire into all questions relating to British and foreign colonization and emigration.

(6) To publish a journal of the proceedings of the Society with a summary of geographical information.

(7) To form a collection of maps, charts, geographical works of reference and specimens of raw materials and commercial products.

Such objectives are exactly what one might have expected of the Manchester business men of that day, but it is significant that hidden away amongst the commercial aims, was a declared intention to encourage the teaching of geography and it was in this sphere that the Society was to make its biggest contribution.

II

The Eli Sowerbutts era 1884–1904

From the outset the Society revealed the dynamic personalities of its leaders. On 4 February 1885, little more than a week after the inaugural meeting, the Council held its first meeting, and confirmed the appointment of H. M. Steinthal and J. F. Hutton as Chairman and Vice-Chairman respectively. In their election one sees recognition of their long-held and steadfast belief in a Manchester Geographical Society, but the choice of these two prominent business men, the latter then President of the Chamber of Commerce, was to be amply justified in the sequel for both gave long and unstinted support and can justifiably claim a large share in the Society's very rapid rise to prominence.

At the first Council, Eli Sowerbutts became the full-time Secretary. The selection of this erstwhile accountant who for several years had been an indefatigable worker behind the scenes, enthusiastically urging on the other founders, was to shape the destiny of the Society and to drive it surgingly forward and upward in a manner that can scarcely have been imagined even by the most optimistic. The history of the next twenty years represents a personal triumph for this remarkable man.

Having appointed the necessary officers, the Council proceeded to set up sub-committees to undertake the detailed planning. A General Purposes Committee, in particular, received instructions to select an office and a bookroom at a rental not exceeding £50 per annum, and such were the conditions in those days that on 9 February it was able to accept an offer by the Manchester Fire Insurance Company of two rooms at the top of 44 Brown Street, which thus became the first official home of the Society.

Though these premises at the corner of King Street (now demolished) were later described by J. H. Reed as 'old fashioned' and rather more pungently by Eli Sowerbutts as 'attics', they were to see the Society prosper to a remarkable extent in the next ten years; at the end of this time pressure of growing possessions made new quarters imperative, but in the first few years there was room enough for the simple administration and for the smaller discussion meetings.

The Council, however, concentrated its attentions on the larger meetings and these soon began to bring famous explorers, travellers and missionaries to Manchester, even though members themselves contributed papers of high value. In February 1885, whilst Sowerbutts was moving into his new office and making contact with the geographical world, the Council arranged for A. Arnold, a local member of Parliament, to speak on 'Our Commercial Opportunities in Western Asia'. Dealing with an area very much in the public eye, it received an ovation from the Press, the *Manchester Guardian* going so far as to write that it was a good example of what lectures ought to be, and amply justified the existence of the Society.

Since the Society had no suitable quarters of its own, Sowerbutts had to avail himself of any public hall he could find. For the first few months meetings varied from place to place until, after settling temporarily at the Athenaeum, they took place regularly at the Memorial Hall in Albert Square. For Arnold's lecture the Society gladly accepted the offer of the Chemistry Theatre at Owen's College where two hundred seats were reserved for members and the remaining two hundred were thrown open to the public. On this occasion Dr. Greenwood, Vice-Chancellor of the Victoria University, occupied the Chair, and in the course of the proceedings announced that His Grace the Duke of Devonshire had consented to become the President of the Society. That so learned a man as the Chancellor of the Victoria University should accept nomination not only witnessed the persuasive powers of Dr. Greenwood himself, but also symbolizes the standing of the new Society and the very real support given it in academic circles.

Subsequently lectures took place at Cheetham and Salford Town Halls and the Athenaeum, being held monthly as far as possible. Some idea of the range of topics can be gained from the titles in that first year: 'The Results of Exploration between lake Nyassa and the Indian Ocean 1880–84' by the Rev. Chauncey Maples; 'Canada and the Great North West' by Professor Boyd Dawkins; 'Siam and the Shan States' by J. A. Bryce; 'Northern India and Afghanistan' by Major-General Sir J. Goldschmid; 'British Interests in East and Equatorial Africa' by H. H. Johnston; 'British

Honduras' by Lieutenant Colonel E. Rogers, and 'The Great North-West; the Pacific Slope' by the Rev. S. A. Steinthal. Large and enthusiastic audiences testified to the popularity of such fare, and the local newspapers gave considerable space to reports and comments in the work of the Society.

Whilst thus consolidating its position locally, the Society started to make itself known to kindred bodies abroad, Sowerbutts entering into active correspondence with their officials and arranging for them to contribute journals and geographical information. The Continental organizations apparently bore no resentment towards their new rivals for, as early as April, nineteen had sent their magazines. On 2 March 1885, the Council gave further impetus to this development by the election of distinguished Honorary Members such as Count Ferdinand de Lesseps, Lord Aberdare and Commander V. L. Cameron, R.N. In the months that followed, many other illustrious names were added to the roll.

The first Council followed up the enquiries of the Provisional Committee into a journal by appointing a Publicity Committee consisting of the Chairman, Vice-Chairman, Professor Boyd Dawkins, Rev. L. C. Casartelli, J. H. Nodal and the Hon. Secretaries, with Eli Sowerbutts as Editor. Driving forward with great energy, their deliberations met with such success that the first issue, with sixty-eight pages (and containing the text of three lectures, the Inaugural Address, correspondence, reviews and proceedings) appeared at the end of April 1885, meeting with general approval.

Originally it was intended to issue the *Journal* in monthly parts, but this could never be achieved. For many years it came out quarterly and then after the 1914–18 war, as a single annual volume. To read these early magazines is to realize the purposeful resolve of the founders and the indefatigable ardour of the editor, which led to the achievement of a high and mature standard within a few months of the Society's birth.

The desire to collect the latest information, particularly that of use to merchants and exporters, soon led to the election of Corresponding Members all over the world, who sent back reports on exploration and current developments in their area. These despatches, together with data from missionaries, came to form the material for smaller meetings in the Library which were attended with considerable enthusiasm.

Having achieved so much so soon, it would not have been surprising if the society had been content to rest on its laurels. Instead, burning missionary enthusiasm led the Council to take a lively interest in the work being carried on by the Royal Geographical Society in an attempt to rectify the deplorable state of geographical education in this country. Whatever other virtues the British may possess, they have never been outstanding for their education policy, and geography had fared worse than most other subjects in the early nineteenth century. Then, in the sixties and at the insistence of Francis Galton, the Royal Geographical Society made strenuous efforts to improve the standard of instruction by awarding medals on the results of special examinations. The scheme ran for some sixteen years, but eventually failed because of apathy on the part of most schoolmasters and because of dull, inaccurate and obsolescent textbooks. At this juncture Douglas Freshfield intervened energetically and caused an enquiry into the whole question of geographical education to be set on foot. In 1884 John Scott Kettie was appointed Inspector of Geographical Education with instructions to visit the Continent to collect characteristic textbooks, maps, globes and other appliances and to investigate the teaching methods employed.

In the early seventies attempts made to induce the Universities to recognize the subject in their curricula by the Royal Geographical Society were politely flouted. The subject, it was assured, was beneath the dignity of university recognition and was only suited for elementary schools. At this we need not be surprised when we examine the geographical literature of the period. It is true that in certain of our great narratives of exploration—Franklin, Ross, Darwin, Bates, Wallace, Livingstone, etc., the scientific side of the subject was dealt with seriously, but the few works which existed on general geography were entirely descriptive, no attempt was made to show the relations which existed between the various distributions over the earth's surface and the interaction between these and the human beings who had to adapt themselves to the geographical conditions or modify them for the benefit of humanity.

The textbooks of the mid-nineteenth century contained dreary lists of names and little more—names of capes, names of bays, mountains, rivers, towns, all completely isolated as if they had no sort of relationship to each other, nor to human beings who had to live and move and have their being amongst them. No wonder geography was rejected and despised by the universities if this kind of thing was all it had to say for itself. Then there were the featureless atlases and wall maps, the value of which was estimated mainly by the number of names which they contained. Visual aids were regarded as too childish for serious educational or scientific purposes. Field work was undreamed of.

When these burning questions were raised in council on 13 April 1885, an Education Committee consisting of Professors Boyd Dawkins, Core and Ward (of Owens College), Samuel Dill (High Master of Manchester Grammar School), the Rev. L. C. Casartelli (of St. Bede's College) and Canon R. Holgate Brown was appointed to enquire into the local position. Meeting on 11th May, the Committee immediately instituted enquiries into methods used on the Continent and America, involving the aid of Sir Henry Roscoe and Signor Bodio for this purpose. They also considered the report made by Scott Kettie.

Realizing only too clearly the need for drastic action, a conference of teachers was promulgated, but this was eventually abandoned in favour of sending out a questionnaire which would reach a greater number of those concerned. In October 1885, the Committee circulated a document to some thirty educational establishments of various kinds asking:

(1) How much time is allotted per week to geography, and is it taught as a separate subject?

(2) Are any prizes offered for proficiency?

(3) What methods and appliances are used; in particular what textbooks and maps?

(4) What are the special hindrances to the thorough and scientific teaching of the subject?

(5) In the case of Institutions, what provision is there for geographical lectures?

The replies showed that geography was taught for an average of about two hours per week to all children in primary and middle-class schools, generally as a separate subject. Few schools encouraged its study by awarding prizes, though a small number awarded them on combined marks for grammar, history and geography. With one or two notable exceptions there appeared to be a total absence of appliances other than textbooks and maps the standard of which left very much to be desired. In those schools where globes, sand-models, pictures, specimens etc. were employed, it could be directly attributed to the enthusiasm of individual teachers. One institution, founded at a cost of £40,000, just replied 'We do not teach geography.' At Owens College, Political Geography was taught in connection with History, at both the elementary and advanced levels. Physical Geography was taught under the head of Physiography as a separate subject and used as an introduction to Geology.

The hindrances suggested were many and various, though the majority of replies could be described under the general heading of 'lack of interest'. A minority adopted a less negative attitude and complained of (a) the want to sufficient support in Universities and schools generally, (b) the consequent shortage of trained teachers, (c) the competition exercised by established subjects and (d) the extreme paucity and low quality of teaching aids.

The replies constituted a severe indictment of the teaching of geography, and about the only consolation the Society could derive lay in the fact that the replies from the Grammar Schools, the High School for Girls and St. Bede's College revealed that Manchester possessed three institutions where instruction in the subject clearly exceeded the average, and that Principal Greenwood strongly favoured the appointment of a Professor or Lecturer in Geography.

Sowerbutts soon realized that here was a problem into which the Society could well get its teeth, and in so doing amply justify its existence, a view shared by the enlightened Casartelli. Whilst the Committee was strengthened by the addition of E. J. Broadfield and N. Wardle, Sowerbutts visited the Royal Geographical Society to discuss with the Marquis of Lorne (who had succeeded Lord Aberdare as President) the best way for Manchester to further the work being done in London. During the course of the interview, provisional arrangements were made for the 'Exhibition of Geographical Appliances' (which had been organized by the Royal Geographical Society to display a representative selection of the materials collected by Kettie in the course of his continental travels) to be brought to Manchester after it had been shown in the metropolis.

Whilst the work and interests of the Society had expanded with a speed that even the most optimistic had not foreseen, Sowerbutts found time to institute small fortnightly meetings in the Library at the top of the Brown Street building for discussions and the reading of short papers. This new departure typified the Secretary's practical approach to his subject and aimed at making full use of the Society's resources, both material and intellectual, to create a body of informed opinion and a corpus of knowledge which would be freely available to merchants and teachers. The members attending the meetings soon came to form an inner circle of great strength and value, and gave the Society a personality that could never have been achieved solely from the inevitably more formal monthly lectures. An additional factor is that, being essentially a local body whose members often met in the course of ordinary business, a social side complementary to the geographical, began to grow up and to give the Society a character all its own.

Thus the first year ended with a record of solid achievement, with hopes and prospects running high. The only cloud was that of finance, which was to be expected in view of the need to equip the Library and Offices, and a slightly sombre note is struck by the appointment of a collector of overdue subscriptions from those whose enthusiasm exceeded their willingness to give financial support. Council realized only too well that to carry through existing plans and to introduce new ideas then under active consideration would involve a much heavier expenditure than they could afford, and as a first step they urged the need for raising the membership above the 383 on the books at 31 December 1885, thus originating an appeal that has echoed down the years. The Society has never suffered from a dearth of ideas. Indeed, the records show that many projects far in advance of current practice have had to be shelved indefinitely for want of funds. From time to time benefactors helped the Society out of difficulties, but there has never been money enough to build up an endowment fund. In the last analysis, membership is the key to financial stability, and though the next few years saw it rise steadily to a maximum of 873 at the end of 1890, the resources of the region in geographers seem to have been overstrained and a gradual decline set in which persisted, with occasional small recoveries, until 1942 by which time it was under 300. The lack of enthusiasm which caused the failure of 1880 has continued to thwart the Society and to baulk it on the threshold of success ever since.

The large lectures continued the following year with unabated enthusiasm, audiences of 600 being not unusual, but the main effort was in the educational field. To demonstrate to local authorities the considerable resources which could be made available to improve the teaching of the subject, part of the Royal Geographical Society 'Exhibition of Geographical Educational Appliances' was brought to Manchester, after its display in London, in the autumn of 1885. With it were blended material provided locally, such as specimens of relief models made by the High School for Girls, maps published by Messrs John Heywood of Manchester and Messrs George Philips of Liverpool, and exhibits loaned by members. Maps formed the principal feature.

The Exhibition, open for a month, was housed in the Art Gallery in Mosley Street, where it was opened on 16 March 1886 by the Mayor, Alderman Goldschmidt, in the unavoidable absence of Lord Napier.

The work of foreign cartographers clearly outstripped that of their British counterparts, German maps taking the palm for the extreme delicacy of their engraving, French maps for their hill shading. The *Manchester Guardian* went so far as to write that 'the constant use of the map is the beginning of wisdom. We are confronted by the deplorable badness of English map making (we accept the Ordnance Survey which is only intolerably slow) and of English school atlases in particular.'

Though the appeal of the exhibition was largely visual, its value was greatly increased by a series of seventeen addresses on subjects connected with geographical education. Dr. Greenwood, Vice-Chancellor of the Victoria University, which existed side by side with Owens College, and a staunch supporter of the Society over many years, delivered the first on 'The Teaching of Geography and the Proper Distribution of its Several Branches', giving a clear account of how the subject was regarded in the more advanced academic circles of that day.

Greenwood argued:

> If I am right in claiming for geography, as a branch of study, the dignity and importance which I think its due, it will follow that its title to be ranked as an academical subject has its roots in something much deeper and more abiding than the accidents of a season or the attention drawn towards it either by the interests of commerce or by the attractions of a period of geographical discovery, ready as we may be to admit the force of these considerations and to take advantage of their influence.

This paper deserves to be better known and the theories propounded should be recorded in any history of the development of geography in this country, particularly his plea for systematic and also regional geography.

A paper by Scott Kettie on 'Geographical Education on the Continent' summarized the position in this country by saying that

> 'in the universities it has no place whatsoever. It is scarcely better off in our great public schools. While in some middle class schools it has a fairly satisfactory position, in these schools though nominally in the programme, it is shunted into a corner and consists merely in learning a string of names by rote. Happily in our Board Schools its position has greatly improved, and is bound still further to improve, though I must say it seems to me that our elementary teachers have yet much to learn as to the real character of the subject.'

He quoted Germany as the model to be followed. It has twelve university Chairs, whilst the subject was taught in every class of school on a carefully regulated plan and with a wealth of appliances. Most of the teachers had had a regular and careful training. Very few British schools had outstanding teachers, but he named G. Ogilvie of Gordon's Academy as one such and A. Hughes of Manchester Grammar School as another.

Though highly successful in quickening the interest of educational authorities, in showing the progress made abroad, and in driving home the lamentable state of British geography, the

Exhibition burdened the Society with a debt that strained its resources for a number of years. Appeals had to be made to philanthropists, and canvassers were appointed to raise membership on the basis of 10 per cent commission for each new subscription, with 5 per cent if renewed for a second and third year.

Meanwhile the Education Committee continued to urge the school authorities to provide scientific apparatus, however simple, for the teaching of geography, and to provide better textbooks, maps, models, etc. They suggested that the Society should institute special prizes, and that the university should co-operate in the creation of an examining body to grant certificates to approved teachers. They also proposed that lectureships should be established in all universities to build up a body of competent instructors whose knowledge and interest would in time act on the lower schools. More practically, they gave a great deal of help to individual masters, and paid visits to numerous schools and institutions. As a result, both the Union of Lancashire and Cheshire Institutes, and the Yorkshire Union increased their requirements in geography, particularly the commercial aspect, and the Pendleton Mechanics' Institute offered a prize in their Commercial Examination which included geography.

The Royal Geographical Society, on the result of their own investigations, and encouraged by the support of the Manchester and Scottish Societies, approached the Vice-Chancellors of Oxford and Cambridge with a view to setting up organizations there similar to those in Continental universities, and the appointment of Readers or Lecturers in Geography.

They also suggested the establishment at each university of a £100 exhibition for the geographical investigation of an approved district or for prizes. They also informed the President of the Council of Education that they would offer prizes to pupil teachers. The Scottish Geographical Society also instituted prizes for special examinations and for map- and model-making. The long struggle for the recognition of geography had entered its last phase.

At the Annual Meeting of 1885, H. M. Steinthal had retired from the chairmanship of Council for business reasons, his place being taken by Henry Lee, J.P., with Principal J. G. Greenwood as Vice-Chairman. The crusading zeal of the Society, however, continued unabated, and Sowerbutts could read with satisfaction the *City News* report that

> 'the *Journal* of the Manchester Geographical Society is still improving. In the matter of pure science, the publications of the Royal Geographical Society may surpass it, but as regards geography in connection with commerce and the large English trading interests all over the world, our local quarterly is gradually taking the premier place, if it has not already attained it.'

Far from being complacent at this outburst of patriotic pride, Sowerbutts proposed that a series of short lectures should be delivered to form the groundwork of a monograph on the Geography of Lancashire under the headings Prehistoric, Physical, Hydrology, Historical, Natural History including Geology, Climate, Botany and Zoology, Descriptive and Miscellaneous, which are of interest for the light they throw on the methodology of his time.

Towards the end of October, R. E. Dennett delivered a lecture on 'The Congo Question from the Traders' point of View' and made this burning topic highly controversial by accusing both the Foreign and Colonial Offices of neglecting the interests of British traders, the consuls of sending inferior reports, and the missionaries of spreading the liquor traffic. Though it is clear that he overstated his case, his remarks led to lively discussions and to quickened interest in the work of the missionaries themselves.

These friendly arguments in the Library of the Brown Street building between kindred spirits, and the growing quantity of books and magazines being sent from all parts of the world, caused a number of members to form themselves into a working party to delve into the resources of the Society and to lay before members the results of their researches. One of the first tasks was to make a summary of the principal material in the many magazines being received and to publish an index to it in the *Journal*. This feature proved so valuable that other societies copied Manchester's example. Another activity was the selection and preparation of slides for projection by the newly introduced and very popular 'limelight'. It is scarcely necessary to state that the instigator of this group, which assumed the name of The Victorians in honour of the Queen's Jubilee, was Eli Sowerbutts.

Following the financial loss on the Exhibition, the Society had to restrict the scale of its activities and 1887 became a year of consolidation. The increase in membership, though encouraging, failed to keep pace with the aspirations of the Officers and Council, but both the university and the Chamber of Commerce gave the new Society their full support. As Principal Greenwood said 'Manchester was fortunate in having men of leisure, intelligence and the enterprise necessary to carry them abroad; and to bring home again ample return in the way of impressions and valuable information.'

The lectures covered a wide field, both geographical and commercial, and if Africa continued to be the magnetic attraction, there is evidence of a growing awareness of Asiatic trading possibilities; at this time 75 per cent of the produce of Lancashire mills went for export, nearly half of it to India, so that an address such as that by A. R. Colquhoun on the great importance of building a railway from Burma into China to tap a potential market of 100 million souls, aroused great interest.

A minor landmark was achieved on Saturday, 15 January 1887, this being the date of the first address by a lady: Miss M. K. Sturgeon came from Ilkley to speak on 'The Teaching of Elementary Geography' illustrated by a practical lesson. The special significance of this is that whereas the Manchester and Scottish societies admitted women on the same terms as men, the Royal Geographical Society would not face up to granting them even ordinary membership despite the fact that Victoria's Jubilee called attention to the ability of women in high places. In 1892 they invited the famous traveller, Mrs Bishop (*née* Bird) to address them, but she refused to speak to a Society of which she could not become a member, and thus precipitated a crisis which continued with varying degrees of acrimony until 1913 when women were eventually admitted.

The Victorians soon settled down to practical work in the cause of geography and within a short time they had made a useful contribution by preparing eleven special charts showing the distribution of major commodities and manufactures. These charts, together with a tariff map of the world, made a deep impression when they were exhibited at the Manchester Exhibition arranged to celebrate the Queen's Jubilee.

The major event in the intellectual field, however, was the meeting in Manchester of the British Association in 1887. From the report of the Society's delegate, it is apparent that the organization of the Geographical Section left much to be desired, there being insufficient time for the proper discussion of the many topics raised, and many papers having to be read as abstract. Two subjects in which the Society took particular interest ('Geography in Relation to Education' and 'The Work of the Ordnance Survey') were particularly unfortunate. Nevertheless, a committee was formed to co-operate with the Royal Geographical Society in an endeavour to bring before the authorities at Oxford and Cambridge the advisability of promoting the study of geography by establishing special professorships. The Presidential Address of Section E by Colonel Sir C. Warren, R.E., C.M.G., dealt with the teaching of geography in schools and advocated, amongst other things, that geographical facts should be learned by means of verses set to music! His speech did, however, show that great improvements had been made in Board School instruction even if fee-paying schools still lagged behind. As part of the social activities, Henry Lee, Chairman of Council, gave a garden party at his home, but the Manchester rainfall managed to damp the occasion.

With the autumn, the Society embarked on yet another venture, and, together with members of the affiliated Burnley Literary and Scientific Club, a party of some ninety persons went on an excursion to Preston to inspect the new docks which were of particular interest to Mancunians at that time as the effect of the £1¼ million improvements would have an important bearing on the success of the nearly completed Ship Canal. Whilst in the town, the party also inspected the Cross Street Museum and the Harris Institute.

Shortly afterwards, the interest in educational matters and the excursion venture found a common activity, when, under the leadership of Principal Greenwood, members paid the first of several visits to local libraries and museums to see their geographical resources. In November the Chetham's Library received the Society, and the Librarian (J. E. Tinkler) displayed the treasures under his charge. Subsequently a select bibliography appeared in the *Journal* which drew public attention to the valuable collections already existing in the district. The following year similar visits were made to Peel Park Museum, Manchester Free Reference Library and Liverpool Library and Museum.

During the year the Society heard with great satisfaction that, encouraged by the success that had greeted the Manchester and Scottish societies, the Rev. F. O. Sutton of All Saints' Church, Newcastle, and G. E. T. Smithson had succeeded in founding a similar society known as the Tyneside Geographical Society. Doubtless due to a fellow feeling towards another provincial body, warm ties of friendship grew up and for many years the two societies worked in the closest harmony.

The year ended full of hope. The Society itself had continued to grow in size and its activities had been widely commended, above all in the educational field. With the backing of the Manchester Society the Royal Geographical Society had been encouraged to take action concerning the proposed professorships and the combined activities of four geographical societies had so stirred public opinion that Oxford and Cambridge began to take notice, while King's College London actually appointed H. G. Seeley, F.R.H., to a professorship. Professor H. G. Seeley visited Harpurhey on 16 March 1888 to lecture in the Conservative Hall under the auspices of the Gilchrist Educational Trust on 'Water and its Action in Land Shaping'. The advance notices earnestly invited all to attend as such a rare intellectual treat might not occur again for a long period of time. Admission was one penny!

More practically, the inspired teaching of Dr. Casartelli and his staff at St. Bede's College in the realm of commercial geography was beginning to attract national attention. The officers of the Society, too, were being consulted by a number of schools as to the best type of equipment. The debt from previous years had been reduced; meetings attracted good audiences; the communications from a rapidly increasing number of foreign correspondents brought stimulating new facts; the *Journal* had been hailed as a substantial contribution to geographical knowledge.

Greatly encouraged, the Council entered 1888 with confidence. To improve the Society's service to members, they began the publication of a monthly pamphlet entitled *Notice of Meetings* which gave details of future speakers and their subjects, and also information on general items of exploration and other geographical matters. One such item, in March, informed members that the curator of Bergen Museum, a Mr. Nansen, was about to undertake a journey of exploration in Greenland, which he proposed to cross from one side to the other. Later in the year a visit to Booth Hall was announced with the comment 'A Glee Party will be in attendance'.

At this juncture the Society left the Athenaeum and the next few years held its main lectures at the Memorial Hall in Albert Square. The emphasis in these lectures still remained on Africa and culminated in a conference on the Nyassa Question following similar gatherings in London and Edinburgh in response to reports of continued slavery in East Africa. The Conference took place in the Mayor's Parlour on 18 May 1888 with Dr. Greenwood and, later, Mark Stirrup in the chair. Many distinguished visitors attended, including Bishop Smythies, Dr. A. L. Bruce (Livingstone's son-in-law) and representatives from other geographical societies, the Anti-Slavery Society and many missionaries and traders.

After hearing eyewitness accounts of the commercial and missionary difficulties and of the depredation by the Arabs in the North and having heard various speakers express their concern at the way in which, for political considerations, the Government had allowed British traders to be squeezed out by the Germans from the paramount position they had achieved by their own initiative until we had no port between Aden and Natal, the conference decided that the Government would take no active measures until forced to do so by public opinion. Consequently, a memorial was despatched to the Marquis of Salisbury urging that the Zambesi, like the Congo and the Niger, should be made free to the flags of all nations so that the interior should not be deprived of the only existing means of free access and of the introduction of Christian civilization and commerce by any one nation; and that the Government should take steps to check the increase of slavery in the Nyassa district due to Arab slave traders.

In November, Commander V. L. Cameron, R.N., C.B., the Society's first Honorary Member, appeared unexpectedly in Manchester and spoke movingly on the cruel slavery still rampant in Africa. The matter arose again a month later in an address by Sir James

Marshall, late Chief Justice of the Niger District, the Rev. Laurence Scott of Denton (an experienced missionary) and Commander Cameron entering into the discussion. Bishop Vaughan then read a letter from the fiery-hearted Cardinal Lavigerie, Archbishop of Carthage and Algiers, introducing the Anti-Slavery Crusade inaugurated by Pope Leo XIII in an attempt to overcome a wanton loss of life estimated at over a million souls each year. A resolution of support was addressed to the Pope and his reply is preserved amongst the Society's archives. The result of so much public outcry, for Manchester was by no means a lone voice, was seen in the Anglo-German Blockade of the East African Coast by Admirals Deinhard and Fremantle.

Whilst this more exciting activity continued, the less spectacular work went on unabated. The regular library meetings provided an outlet for discussion; the Victorians worked on their slide collection and combed incoming journals for new information; the Council gave thought to setting up a commercial museum; the local excursions became an established feature of the summer; the *Journal* published in April (vol. 3, pts 7–12) contained illustrations for the first time in the form of line blocks.

So far as museums were concerned, Casartelli had for a long time been a strong advocate for making specimens of various products available for students to see and handle for themselves. Eli Sowerbutts, as practical as ever, staunchly supported him. In Commander Cameron they found another of their persuasion for the last-mentioned had done his best to found a geographical society in London a few years previously, failing only for want of money and was now hoping that his ideas would eventually be realized by the Imperial Institute.

The suggestions of these three pioneers were further strengthened by the opening, on 8 June 1888, of the Manchester Museum's new building at the university. From 1869 to 1888 Professor Boyd Dawkins had acted as curator, and under his care the collections had grown until more space became an urgent need, and more extensive galleries were obtained by public subscription helped by a £28,000 grant from The Whitworth Legatees.

After a programme of local excursions to such places as the Ship Canal, Boggart Hole Clough and Moston, in September about thirty members made a five-day visit to Antwerp, Brussels and

Waterloo. Naturally, envious eyes were cast on the fine Commercial Museum at Antwerp. In Brussels contact was made with the Royal Belgian Geographical Society whose Secretary courteously conducted the visitors round the city.

The year 1889 produced no special highlights, but the membership continued to grow encouragingly, and the Society settled down to a series of discussions in which commerce and unrest in Africa bulked big. The large lectures, now almost exclusively in the Memorial Hall, broke away from Africa towards a better balanced programme which included China, Fernando Po, the Trans-Siberian Railway and Florida. L. H. Grindon brought a fresh approach to the subject with his talk on 'The Geographical Distribution of Plants' and J. H. Silberbach kept the educationalists satisfied with 'The Teaching of Elementary Commercial Geography in Primary and Secondary Schools'.

In this change of emphasis one can detect the influence of the geographically minded element at the expense of the commercial. Many of the original business men associated with the foundation had little time to devote to the Society after the first few years, but they had seen it through its teething stages and had brought it into such prominence that it gradually became a focus for the geographers in the district. Advanced geography however, was slow in taking root in the Manchester area, and the Society continued in the hands of amateur enthusiasts with quite a strong social side as well.

It is interesting to note that three active members published books in 1889, Cardwell's *Introduction to the Study of Commercial Geography*; Casartelli's *Notes on Commercial Geography* and Alfred Hughes' *First Book on Geography*. At the same time the Victorians began to analyse the contents of all the foreign journals and to publish a tabulated bibliography in the *Journal*, a feature of great value which was soon copied by other organizations. In addition, they prepared maps to illustrate the lectures and talks, and themselves established a panel of 'geographical missionaries' to give popular addresses outside the Society with the intention of extending its influence and bringing its interests and facilities before the general public. This is another example of the practical approach to the subject, and as will be seen it developed into an important aspect of the Society's work, creating a tradition that has been maintained ever since. In April of that same year, 1889, Mackinder made a separate attempt to popularize geography by giving a free course of lectures in Ancoats, his efforts meeting with substantial success.

The summer outings continued to have a social side at least equal to the geographical. Trips included the Technical School in Princess Street, Ardwick Museum and the General Post Office in Manchester, and Whalley, Stoneyhurst and the Ship Canal at Eastham further afield. Rather more scientifically, a visit was made to Chat Moss. The main attraction however lay in Paris, and a party of fifty members crossed the Channel and attended the International Geographical Congress. On 9 August, a party went from the hotel in Rue Triton to the Elysée Palace where they were received by the President of the Republic. In the little ceremony that followed, two young ladies, the Misses Dean and Edmondson, presented the President with the inevitable 'handsome bouquet' and Miss Law handed him the first four volumes of the *Journal* bound in full morocco.

With the autumn, Africa again returned to the Syllabus, with Governor Moloney speaking on cotton interests in West Africa. He also delivered a lecture on 'Native Melodies of West Africa', a novel aspect of geography. The two most distinguished speakers, however, were Joseph Thomson of Morocco fame, and Prince Kropotkin who discussed 'What Geography Ought to Be'. In October, a joint meeting with the Manchester Statistical Society listened to a paper on 'Manufacturing Processes in Relation to Health'.

The New Year 1890 received fitting recognition when members living in north and north-west Manchester, under the leadership of Samuel Ogden, arranged an 'At Home' in Cheetham Town Hall. Slides of Greece, music, dancing and 'other enjoyments' were provided. On the more serious side, however, the Society had the good fortune to welcome H. J. Mackinder, the newly appointed Reader in Geography at Oxford. He spoke on the 'Necessity of a Thorough Teaching in General Geography as a Preliminary to the Teaching of Commercial Geography', a subject very much to the taste of the more academically minded members, and one indicating that the teaching of geography was about to take a great stride forward towards modern methodology. He stressed the fact that commercial geography, which bulked so large in educational literature and the Presidential Addresses of the British Association, was after all only one of the many applications of geography proper, and that a sound training in the latter was absolutely essential.

In March, Douglas Freshfield, the outstanding Hon. Secretary of the Royal Geographical Society, came to lecture on the Caucasus, an event doubly interesting to members in view of Herman Woolley's explorations there.

Meanwhile, Mackinder's words seem to have fallen on fertile ground, for shortly afterwards, Mark Stirrup, a keen geologist, advanced the cause of physical geography with the first of several papers on Languedoc, in which he dealt with the denudation and the régime of the rivers.

Mackinder had also underlined the importance of local studies in geography, and the need for the proper appreciation of maps. This point too seems to have been taken up, for later in the year the Society listened to a description of a layered contour map on a scale of two inches to the mile, specially prepared by F. D. King of Bradford for the teaching of local geography. Councillor Joseph Harding of Preston also gave an enthusiastic talk on the importance and opportunity of local studies. The members themselves maintained an interest in the district with visits to Liverpool Docks ('living commercial geography') and reservoirs in the Ashworth valley and near Hebden Bridge.

Sowerbutts, with his intense love of children, realized that though the battle for the recognition of geography would have to be fought at adult level, it would be a rewarding long-term investment to capture the enthusiasm of the younger generation whilst they were still at the formative stage. A direct appeal was therefore made to them in March 1890 when some 150 slides were shown to an audience of 500 scholars at the Lower Mosley Street School—the choice suggests the influence of S. A. Steinthal. The meeting proved a great success as well it might in those days of uninspired teaching before the cinema and complicated visual aids. One suspects however that this form of activity roused enthusiasm for the 'new geography' as a soft option.

H. M. Stanley was not a very popular personality in the geographical world as a whole, but his reception on his various visits to Manchester was invariably enthusiastic, that in June 1890 being no exception to the rule. Doubtless as the result of the part he had played nearly six years previously in the events leading up to the foundation, the Society received him with special pleasure. On 20 June he addressed a brilliant and packed audience in the Free Trade Hall on his expedition to rescue Emir Pasha, and the next day he was made an honorary freeman of the city. A deputation from the Society attended the ceremony and S. A. Steinthal as Chairman of the Council, presented an illuminated address in honour of the explorer. After luncheon he was taken on a tour of inspection along the nearly completed Ship Canal as far as Barton, and in the evening he attended a civic reception with 1300 guests.

Stanley's visit naturally stimulated interest in Africa, and with the Heligoland exchange fresh in mind, a symposium was held in November on the present position in Nyassaland. Addresses were delivered by the Bishop of Salford, Archdeacon Chauncey, Rev. D. Kerr Cross of the Free Church of Scotland Mission and J. W. Mair, Manager of the African Lakes Company.

Other activities however were not forgotten. Following Mackinder's remarks on maps, Colonel H. T. Crook started his important campaign for the improvement of Ordnance Survey maps, a theme he was to pursue with great perseverance for many years to come. To read his remarks today, when Ordnance Survey maps are a byword for perfection, and used by all and sundry as a matter of course, brings home vividly the progress that has been achieved in the last sixty years or so, much of the improvement owing something to Colonel Crook's work.

In 1890 many Ordnance maps were hopelessly obsolete, for example the only available sheet of Eastbourne was dated 1813, presumably a product of the Napoleonic wars. Prices were unreasonably high. Worst of all, the sales service was hopelessly inadequate and even if the required map could be found, delivery delays were excessive. As a result, the only readily purchasable maps of the country came from the presses of private publishers who had taken advantage of the situation to the best of their limited resources. It is interesting to find that the Survey subsequently adopted many of the remedies suggested by Crook.

Casartelli, too, entered the lists from a slightly different angle and gave yet another demonstration of his advanced ideas concerning geography when he delivered what must surely be one of the earliest papers on Microclimatology: 'Notes of Manchester Rainfall 1878–1889'. Gustav Jacoby kept alive commercial interests with a paper in the old tradition on British trade with Algeria, Tunisia and the Sahara.

Nor was the educational aspect overlooked. Dr. H. R. Mill, for example, visited Brown Street to repeat his lecture to the British Association on the teaching of geography in Russia. More important though was the issuing by the Education Committee of a second questionnaire to assess the progress achieved during the last five years. It revealed that the Owens College had instituted evening lectures on commercial history and geography in preparation for the Victoria University's commercial certificate, whilst the repeated requests for a lectureship in Geography had met with a modest degree of success inasmuch as H. Spencer Wilkinson, M.A., had been appointed Lecturer in Commercial Geography. The Manchester School Board had introduced a course of lectures on commercial geography too. The Manchester Chamber of Commerce had introduced both general and commercial geography into its scheme for certificates. Cardwell, who had conducted a course in geography over a period of six years at St. Bede's, had gained a considerable local reputation and had been invited to deliver a course on the all too popular commercial aspect of the subject at the Harris Institute, Preston. A few schools had been inspired to set up geographical museums and these had been established at the Manchester and Hulme Grammar Schools and at St. Bede's. Gradually, too, new and better textbooks and apparatus were coming into use.

The replies showed however that some schoolmasters were still uncertain as to what geography included and as to where they should aim. One school wrote that it had not been found possible to allot sufficient time for geography owing to the competition of other subjects more suitable for female education.

It was clear however that the initial enquiries, and particularly the exhibition of teaching aids, had achieved their purpose, and so a further list of the latest materials available was published with the report. In general the Society felt that progress, if slow, was at least in the right direction. The *Manchester Guardian*, on the other hand, felt impatient and stated that the Society should close down as it had not obtained the appointment of a Professor at Owens College.

The Council were impressed by the success of the scheme for prizes adopted by the Royal Geographical Society and decided to take similar action and to institute prizes for competition amongst all children not above the seventh standard in Lancashire, Cheshire and Yorkshire schools. Boyd Dawkins, Core and Casartelli were appointed examiners, and for the first competion set as subject 'The Geography of Lancashire and Cheshire' including such questions as 'Describe briefly the structure of the Lancashire and Cheshire plain' which the entrants, all under 13 years of age, must have found rather stiff going.

The prize idea was catching, and Messrs. George Philip offered a book prize and Theodore Gregory, the Society's Hon. Auditor, provided a special award for an essay by any member of the Society on 'The Commercial Products of Central Africa and the Best Methods of Developing a Trade in them with Europe'. This last was subsequently awarded to J. H. Reed, the Hon. Secretary of the Victorians.

With so much activity, it is not surprising that the membership figures grew appreciably, and the statistics at the end of 1890 show that they had in fact reached their peak, with a total membership of 893, of which 586 were ordinary members. Nevertheless, the officers held the opinion that Greater Manchester should be capable of producing many more, and that this accretion would make possible some of the schemes which had had to be shelved for want of finance. Thus in October 1890 we find Steinthal and Sowerbutts leading a deputation to the Mayor of Rochdale in an attempt to extend the membership in that town.

By 1891 the general pattern of the Society's work had become clear. The main group activity took the form of seventeen or eighteen lectures in the Memorial Hall, most of them dealing with a general regional approach and with a strong accent on trading conditions in deference to the business element among members. Next in popularity came the summer outings which were taken very seriously but which contained so much of a social nature, that the frivolous referred to them as 'Sowerbutts' picnics'. Only a relatively small group attended the library meetings, but these were the real geographical enthusiasts, amongst them the Victorians.

The latter had formed themselves into a lecture panel, and their services were in increasing demand. Then there were the few officers and Council who were fighting for improvement in the general condition of geographical education in the country as a whole and the local area in particular. Lastly there were a few individual enthusiasts such as Crook with his Ordnance Survey maps, Casartelli and Sowerbutts with their museums.

In 1891 the commercial aspect received attention from men such as Professor Vambéry of Budapest on 'British Trade in Central Asia', Alvan Millson on 'Industrial and Commercial Features of the Lagos Area', and J. E. Budgett Meakin on the foreign commerce of Morocco, the last topic exciting considerable interest as the export of textiles there from Manchester and Glasgow employed 7500 looms and 225,000 spindles. Special attention however was focused on India, to which three lectures and several communicative papers were devoted.

At one of the Library meetings, Sowerbutts drew attention to the very real contributions being made to geography by newspapers and periodicals, not only by means of up-to-date telegraphic reports from all over the world but also by their good quality illustrations; in this last respect *Le Temps* received special commendation. In this connection it would be interesting to trace the connection between the introduction of what are now known as 'visual aids' and the increasing popularity of geography during the last years of the nineteenth century and the first decade of the twentieth. Sowerbutts went on to point out how considerable geography could be learned from the articles, letters and reports in the *Manchester Guardian* alone, and how the greater initiative of the Americans enabled them to go so far as to publish a series of articles such as one on 'Physical Geography' by Professor Shaler.

More practically still, J. P. Thompson, Hon. Secretary of the Royal Geographical Society of Australia, and a noted explorer, who was a good friend of the Society, sent an appeal for travellers to make more honest and accurate observations on their journeys as maps with incorrect details wrought untold harm, leading to bitter controversies and even to litigation. This same year brought a lecture on 'Astronomy in Relation to Geography' by Thomas Weir of the Manchester Astronomical Society which proved so popular that it had to be repeated.

The summer outings, though following the customary pattern, were more numerous than before, and culminated in an organized tour through Normandy to Paris, whence Steinthal, Sowerbutts and a few more went on to the Geographical Congress at Berne. Another manifestation of this social side is recorded in the *Journal* for 1892 which describes the Christmas party organized for members' children by the Victorians. The account recaptures the scene quite vividly: 'Lantern views of localities in various parts of the world and some other slides were shown to the great delight of the young people. Games and little romps diversified the evening.' Here we have the indelible pen of Eli Sowerbutts. One wonders what the 'other slides' were, and it seems probable from a search through the Society's 'miscellaneous' drawers, that they were of incidents in popular Victorian ballads such as 'Sally in our alley' er from Dickensian novels like *The Old Curiosity Shop* posed by live models and coloured by hand.

During the summer in June 1891, a special meeting was held in Stockport at the request of several residents in that town with a view to encouraging membership. This eventually led to a Stockport branch with meetings of its own, though the venture did not last many years. Shortly afterwards news came that a larger number of recruits had been made to the cause by the foundation of a Liverpool Geographical Society largely through the initiative of Staff Commander Dubois Phillips, R.N., and with the Earl of Derby as President. The Manchester Society however ended the year with the sad news of the death of the Duke of Devonshire, its own President.

In December the Education Committee gave careful consideration to the financial aspects of appointing a Lecturer in Geography at Owens College. Eventually it was agreed that the Society would subscribe £50 per annum towards his stipend if the Royal Geographical Society would guarantee a similar sum and the College the remainder. The scheme received approval and Owens College subsequently presented a short list of two candidates— J. J. Cardwell or H. Yule Oldham. The Society replied that either man was acceptable. When in February 1892 a lecture by Nansen on 'The North Pole' was arranged in co-operation with Owens College, Dr. Ward was able to comment on the close connection between the College and the Society and to announce that through the joint action of the Manchester Geographical Society, the Royal Geographical Society and the College, arrangements had been made for a lectureship in branches of geographical knowledge not hitherto taught. The appointment of H. Yule Oldham as Lecturer in Political Geography was announced to the Society on the 30 March. The second hurdle on the way to a Chair of Geography had been passed.

Nevertheless, the Council persevered with their policy of promoting the interest of Geography at lower levels and extended their examinations for prizes and certificates to include not only schools, but Mechanics' Institutes and evening classes in Lancashire, Cheshire and Yorkshire, thereby attracting 320 applications, though only a third sat the examination. Boyd Dawkins, Core and Casartelli, however, set rather a high standard considering the 15 years 3 months average age of the entrants and the report of the examiner suggested that many of the candidates were out of their depth.

The Society's visitor (Eli Sowerbutts) attended many primary schools and reported a great improvement in teaching methods, even though a few schools persistently lagged behind. Secondary schools were less satisfactory, some continuing to regard geography as a subject of little importance. The delegate to the British Association at Edinburgh, confirmed the generality of these views.

The ordinary lectures of 1892 continued to show the almost inevitable division into commercial and academic geography. At a joint meeting with the Chamber of Commerce, Mounteney Jephson, one of Stanley's expedition, lectured on 'Trade Prospects in Uganda', a talk described at the time as a first-rate piece of commercial geography. The academically minded won a resounding victory with Delmar Gordon on 'The Early Discovery of Australia', and a series of lectures on the relationship of geography to the more exact sciences, such as geology, meteorology, zoology, etc. Moreover a number of appeals were made for an improvement in the quality of data brought back from the field; though the main features of the continents were known, much specialized and accurate work still remained to complete the picture.

(This meeting subsequently caused the Council to send a delegation to Lord Egerton, the Archbishop of Westminster, Sydney Keymer and the Secretary to the Foreign Office, to press for the expansion of trade with Uganda rather than the evacuation then contemplated.)

Local excursions designed to acquaint members with their local region, were very numerous and involved a return visit to Preston Docks whilst the more adventurous went to France, Italy, Germany, the United States, and a party of seventy crossed the North Sea to Norway.

With its work increasing and its reputation expanding in a most encouraging manner, the Society still lacked a President, and the Council gave serious thought to a successor to the late Duke of Devonshire. After considering various local candidates, a suggestion was made that a member of the royal family should be approached. It so happened that Sir Francis de Winton, the Controller and Treasurer of the Household of T.R.H. the Duke and Duchess of York, was a geographer and had been President of Section E of the British Association. Steinthal and Sowerbutts were instructed to visit him to see what could be done. In the event, negotiations proceeded extremely smoothly and in October there came a letter with the highly gratifying news that the Duke of York would be pleased to become President.

Early in 1893, E. G. Ravenstein, then President of Section E of the British Association, spoke to the Society on two burning topics: 'Europe in Africa' and 'Geography in Schools'. In connection with the latter, it is to be remembered that in May of this year the Geographical Association came into being, an organization created by schoolmasters with the direct intention of improving the status of geography in schools, particularly the public and secondary schools. Though still hampered by lack of finance, the Manchester Society welcomed the new body and gave it moral if not practical support. It also entered into closer co-operation with the Imperial Institute by becoming a local branch and with the Royal Geographical Society by becoming a corresponding society.

Whereas the winter 1892–3 is remarkable for the rather small number of lectures, summer excursions formed a big part of the Society's activity and covered not only the geographical features, history, commerce and industries, but also the geology, botany and natural history of the district. It is worth recording that members made a large number of trips abroad during the year. On these foreign visits, members carried letters of introduction to similar institutions on the Continent, which invariably led to most courteous receptions. Thus encouraged, the Society later urged the 1895 International Geographical Conference to lay down a formal procedure for visiting members.

The autumn brought a number of distinguished speakers before the Society. A highlight was the visit in October of Clements Markham, to speak on 'Trade Routes Through the Himalayas'. Interest remained in Asia, for soon after Lord Lamington spoke on 'Siam and Tonquin' and the Earl of Dunmore described 'Journeyings in the Pamirs and Central Asia'.

The Annual Report for 1893 notes that the Burnley Literary and Scientific Club, an affiliated society, had formed a local centre for geographical work. This development appealed to Council and led to the setting up of a special committee of the officers, together with Dentith, Philips and Sheratt, to examine the possibility of extending the Society's work to other towns in the North, and the creation of a Geographical Institute. As a result of their deliberations, local secretaries were soon appointed for Bury and Rochdale, Heywood, Oldham, Preston, Stockport, Urmston and York. Other towns considered were Blackpool and St. Anne's, Huddersfield, Leigh, Southport and Warrington. In the first instance, these branches held no independent activities, but concentrated on the recruitment of new members for their parent body, the secretaries being allowed 10 per cent of all new subscriptions. Unfortunately these satellites never made any measurable progress apart from a short-lived success in Stockport, and after a few years they lapsed.

Far more successful were the Victorians who continued to operate with undiminished zeal. Though they analysed journals and made lantern slides, and even organized a cycling club, their activities turned more and more towards lecturing. Their members spoke on no less than sixty-two occasions, with audiences up to a thousand strong. The lectures excited considerable favourable comment, and their reputation led to calls from as far afield as St. Annes and Newcastle. As a new departure, they embarked on a W.E.A. type of extension lectures, giving a course of five talks on aspects of geography for students in Messrs. Brunner Mond's works at Winnington, near Northwich. At the end of the year, their passionately devoted Hon. Secretary, J. H. Reed, delivered a special Children's Lecture at Owens College on 'From England to Japan'.

Financial worries loomed large in 1894, the Society's tenth year. Lecture expenses had to be carefully watched, and the Chairman of Council had to appeal for further donations to keep the Owens College lectureship going. By the autumn, the situation had become sufficiently critical for the Council to order a reduction in the size of the *Journal* and the preparation of annual estimates, the latter action proving of great worth over the next few years.

Though short of money, the Society's spirits were undimmed. Yule Oldham was making a great success of his appointment, and had even opened his lectures on 'North America' and the 'History of Geographical Discovery' to the public. The excursions were popular, the Victorians were busier than ever; the Stockport branch had been greatly strengthened by the election of Canon Symonds as local chairman and T. H. Rathbone as local hon. secretary and was looking for a hall in which regular Victorian lectures could be delivered throughout the coming winter. The cause of geography in the North was further strengthened by a movement under a Mr. Hedley, to found a geographical society in Bradford.

The most exciting event, however, was that the Council had decided that the attics in Brown Street were too cramped for the volume of work now being undertaken and quite inadequate for the growing collection of books, maps, slides, etc. There was a strong feeling too, that the position the Society had achieved warranted larger and better quarters. Enquiries were set on foot, and the executors of John Ellis offered the Society a lease of the three top flors of an old building in St. Mary's Parsonage at an annual rent of £100.

With finances in a parlous state, some members of Council looked askance at the increased rent, but grumble as they might, they had to admit that there was no alternative. Eventually it was agreed to accept the offer and to carry out the rather extensive repairs. Shortage of funds was no new experience for the Society and somehow money had always been forthcoming in a time of crisis. The only practical course was to act first and then set about providing the money. This the Society did, and introduced the economies mentioned above, and then, by amending the Rules, enabled it to benefit as a 'Registered Literary or Scientific Society'. Lastly, another appeal was launched inviting members to come to the rescue.

The new quarters, looking on the Irwell, and fronting the quiet green of the Parsonage Gardens, conveniently near Deansgate, seemed a veritable palace after the near-squalor of Brown Street. The move itself took place towards the end of 1894 and when the Society's treasures had been set out more attractively than had ever before been possible, the event was celebrated by receptions on 12 December and again on 26 January.

In spite of the inevitable upset and inconvenience, activities continued with scarcely any interruption, particularly those of the Victorians who enjoyed the busiest winter in their whole history, delivering ninety-four lectures and sending speakers as far afield as Liverpool and Hull, Tenby and Newcastle. In addition they gave another series at Winnington and provided a regular programme for the new Stockport branch.

Roughly contemporaneously with the move, there occurred a change of staff at Owens College. In 1874 Yule Oldham left for Cambridge and after a short interregnum in which Cardwell lent assistance, the College authorities appointed A. J. Herbertson to the vacant post. The latter, who became a lifelong friend and staunch supporter of the Society, entered into his new duties with enthusiasm, very soon organizing courses of lectures on cartography, North America and advanced geography as well as an evening series on the 'Principles of Commercial Geography'.

The new rooms, with their better accommodation, gave Sowerbutts renewed vigour and, even if financial considerations dictated fewer lectures in hired public halls, he organized a greatly increased number of library lectures, many of which were delivered by members. He also took the opportunity to indulge his belief in the broad scope of geography, for the subjects ranged from exploration in New Guinea and the Upper Missouri, to the uses of petroleum and the recent discovery of lake-dwellings at Glastonbury. Polar exploration too, began to appear in the syllabus and Leo Grindon introduced the physical aspect with 'The Life History of a Mountain'.

The Victorians, ever enthusiastic and quite irrepressible, were

36

responsible for several social gatherings, and even a musical evening found its way into the programme.

The first two years at Parsonage Gardens probably witnessed the Society at its zenith. Though the finances were precarious, membership was at its peak, its activities more numerous than at any time until 1953, and its influence was being felt throughout the North-west if not throughout the country.

The Society took its work extremely seriously, and at the time was particularly concerned about the activities of the Geographical Section of the British Association where, the Council felt, non-geographers were playing too prominent a part. The other contentious matter was the Ordnance Survey. For some years Colonel Crook had taken every opportunity to castigate that highly inefficient body, and his remarks at the Leeds British Association in 1892 had been largely responsible for the setting up of the Dorrington Committee. This, however, had not achieved great success and the Council watched with interest as the Board of Agriculture set up a Departmental Committee on arrangements for the sale and distribution of Ordnance Survey maps. Early in 1896 it was suggested that Crook should be invited to assist the Committee but the latter obviously considered him too stormy a petrel, though in the course of time nearly all his suggestions came to be adopted.

An incident on an excursion in May 1895 well illustrates the pompous side of the Society. Arrangements had been made through Lord Ellersmere's agent to visit Worsley Hall, but this gentleman though known to be in the immediate neighbourhood at the time of the visit, made no attempt to meet the party. Whereupon, before dissolving, members formally passed a resolution 'that no vote of thanks be passed as the company feels none were due'.

These summer excursions, rather fewer in number than usual, reached a distinctly higher standard with people like Boyd Dawkins leading a party to study the physical geography of the Castleton and Edale Districts, in continuation of a lecture on the area by Colonel Crook, and a trip under Morgan Brierley to explore the physical geography of the Saddleworth district.

The success of the Stockport Branch led, in June 1895, to a Bowdon Committee being set up with the help of Mark Stirrup. About the same time, J. H. Reed, who had long been one of the driving forces behind the Victorians, proposed that the panel should expand its extension lectures on lines similar to the university extension courses and to the successful lectures at Winnington. Unfortunately neither of these projects achieved much success.

More successful, however, was the co-operation between Owens College and the Society due very largely to Herbertson's enthusiasm. The Council gave permission to the college authorities to use the Library for a series of evening lectures to be delivered by Herbertson himself. These began with ten on the Commercial Geography of Eastern Asia before Christmas, and continued into 1896 with others on Polar Exploration, the Highways of Commerce, the Commerce of Africa, etc.

With the College lectures, the Library meetings and the Friday Victorian gatherings the Society's rooms must have been a hive of activity. The energy of the Victorians must have been prodigious for not only did they discharge a heavy programme of outside lectures, maintain the social side of the Society and analyse the 'exchange' journals, but they also prepared maps and made lantern slides: up to 1895 they had, from their lecturing profits, purchased over £70 worth of slides and other apparatus. The dreams of the founders had been amply fulfilled.

For some time the announcements of lectures had included a few short remarks about the speaker and his subject, and this had gradually taken the form of a periodic news sheet. In the autumn of 1895 this blossomed into a regular publication entitled 'Geography: Notices and Notes of the Manchester Geographical Society'. Usually appearing at monthly intervals, and containing short descriptions of future lectures, details of work being undertaken by the Victorians, miscellaneous geographical information of current interest and a children's page with competition questions, the four-page pamphlet continued until shortly after Eli Sowerbutts' death when, its editor lost, and money scarce, it had to be abandoned. The children's competition with successive questions towards an annual prize (awarded at the children's Christmas Party) is typical of Sowerbutts. It is interesting, moreover, to find that Herbertson considered some of the answers so remarkable for their excellence that he borrowed them for display in the Oxford School of Geography.

With 1896, the lecture programme began with an 'African

Month' but subsequently it introduced topics of more scientific interest such as earthquakes and map projections. There is also evidence of an increased interest in local geography for two talks were given on the Rossendale area preparatory to a field visit. The Liverpool meeting of the British Association heard of the Victorians from J. Howard Reed who, in a paper titled 'Practical Geography in Manchester' described Sowerbutts' efforts to popularize geography in the North-west. He told how occasional lecturers had spoken to various local organizations on geographical subjects and how the demand for such talks had grown almost unbelievably, requiring the setting up of a lecture panel. Making full use of the new limelight lanterns, the Victorians had given three hundred lectures in the previous five years to audiences varying from fifty to twelve hundred. A number of the talks had been arranged by local literary and scientific societies, but the majority had been given to the 'working classes', often through the auspices of the Industrial Co-operative Societies and the Free Libraries.

Unfortunately, geography was not making such healthy progress at Owens College. Though Herbertson had made improvements in the accommodation and built up the nucleus of a geographical collection, the academic authorities seem to have had little sympathy with the subject. A report by Herbertson of this time tells how his classes were attended almost exclusively by first year students of the day training department, and that the numbers were reduced by the regulations of the Education Department which excused all the good students. Moreover, of his three main courses, that on practical geography had not been sanctioned, and evening classes on the Commercial Geography of Eastern Asia and two shorter courses, on the Great Ocean Routes and the Commerce of Africa, were held in the Society's rooms.

Herbertson continued: 'Under existing conditions, the work of the geographical lecturer is not very encouraging, and the pecuniary sacrifice he is called on to make is considerable. He only gets the poorer material to work upon owing to the Education Department's regulations and the lack of any University recognition of the subject. . . . The lecturer regrets that under the existing conditions, he is unable to ask for a renewal of his appointment.' Wise in so many other spheres, the University had failed to recognize the genius in Herbertson, and thus forced him to take his brilliance elsewhere.

Meanwhile the youthful Geographical Association had entered the geographical arena, and by 1896 it had representatives in most of the great public schools. Its chief work at this period was a 'Memorial on the Reform of Geography Examinations' which advocated (1) that physical geography should form the basis of teaching and that a general knowledge of the subject should be required in examinations, together with a special study of some selected region and (2) that public examining bodies should adopt the above suggestions to create a common standard which would replace the existing specialized requirements of individual bodies and hence stimulate teaching. This cutting of the Gordian knot excited considerable interest in Oxford, Cambridge and Manchester, and at the last, soon led to the acceptance of geography as one of the pass subjects but too late, however, to retain Herbertson.

The Council of the Society shared Herbertson's frustration, and having seen two outstanding lecturers come and go in so short a spell of years, they decided to withdraw their grant to the University on the grounds that the money could be spent more usefully elsewhere. Thus the lectureship to which A. W. Flux succeeded was unendowed. Incidentally Flux remained barely longer than his predecessors, resigning in 1899.

The year 1897 may be described as a Polar year for many lectures featured the Arctic and Antarctic. Perhaps the most outstanding of these was the return visit of Nansen in February which formed a great occasion for the Society. The lecture took place in the Free Trade Hall with the Victorians, complete with badges, acting as stewards, and, as the official report states with some pride 'Bonnets were not worn by the audience'. Nansen's reception in all parts of the country was extraordinarily enthusiastic but nowhere keener or more hearty than in Manchester, and when, to the strains of the Norwegian National Anthem on the organ, he appeared on the platform, the audience cheered persistently. So many applications for seats were, in fact, received that an overflow meeting packed the nearby Assembly Rooms to hear G. H. Warren, a Victorian, describe the slides as fast as they could be brought from the main meeting. Before the summer break a total of six lectures on the

Arctic had been delivered to the Society out of the sixteen of the full programme.

One of the major activities of the autumn of 1897 took the form of a conference on 'Missionaries and Geography' organized particularly for those ex-missionaries living near Manchester. The idea found its origin in the large correspondence the Society had carried on over many years with missionaries in all parts of the world. The timing of the meeting turned out to be particularly fortunate as the Lady Mayoress herself had once been a missionary and it should be remembered that Cardinal Vaughan, one of the founders, was also a returned missionary. The aim of the conference was to find out how the Society could best help missionaries, and how the great wealth of material they accumulated could be made more readily available. From the discussions on that occasion the great debt of scientists, traders and explorers to missionaries became very plain. For example, the only maps of the Labrador coast available in 1897 were based on surveys made by Moravian agents.

The autumn lectures included a high proportion by members, a silent comment on the Society's financial position, but fortunately the standard did not suffer as there were such men available as Hermann Woolley who could speak on his travels in the Caucasus, and Mark Stirrup who had recently visited Finland, not to mention C. H. Bellamy and Samuel Wells. The year ended with a big lecture in the Free Trade Hall by Sven Hedin, then a young man of thirty-two, famous already in Sweden, but little known in this country though, as one national weekly said: 'We may expect great things from him in the future.'

The position of geography was gradually improving, and in 1897 the Victorians received so many requests for their services, occasioned by a growing interest in the reality of the British Empire, that their activities had to be more strictly controlled, but even then over sixty talks were given. The general interest in geography is shown by references in the *Journal* to geographical societies at Southampton and Cardiff.

In comparison with 1897, 1898 turned out a quieter year. Even though there were as many meetings as before, there were fewer distinguished visitors, and members themselves played a larger role in the syllabus. Finance, of course, provides the explanation, for the Hon. Treasurer announced the sombre fact that expenditure would probably exceed income by as much as £200. Consequently there had to be immediate economies both in the lecture programme and the *Journal*. This, however, was not entirely bad for it resulted in more attention being paid to the Society's collections. The Library presented an insoluble problem, for the number of books caused serious overcrowding, but this could wait on the future. Instead Casartelli and Sowerbutts devoted their energies to building up the 'Native Produce Collection' always so dear to their hearts, which was ultimately to form the basis of the Commercial Museum. The Victorians, never losing faith in their cause, lectured to 20,000 people and heard with satisfaction that the South African Association had been so impressed with their work that they were seconding L. Dede and M. Ray to the panel.

During the autumn several members of the Council were involved in an attempt by country Fellows of the Royal Geographical Society to get representation on the Council of that Society, a campaign that had been gathering momentum for the past few years. The names of S. L. Keymer, E. W. Mellor and Hermann Woolley were proposed, but the Royal Geographical Society refused to countenance the idea. The Tyneside Geographical Society then made representations to have their society officially represented there, but Manchester could not support them as this might imperil the precious independence of the local organizations. These manoeuverings led to strained relations between the Royal Geographical Society and the provincial societies which continued for several years. One effect of this coolness is seen in the approach made by Sowerbutts to Sir F. Abel at the Imperial Institute which resulted in a meeting of delegates from local societies in an attempt to create Museums of Commercial Geography, with special reference to natural products from the Colonies, throughout the country. Though a certain amount of preparatory work was done, the scheme was never carried through, and the local societies arranged their own displays.

Towards the end of the year and the early part of 1899, interest turned towards geographical education, and in a retrospective review Sowerbutts considered the part the Society had played and the extent to which it had achieved its declared objects. He said that scientific and official documents were being studied with great profit at Library meetings, and that at these gatherings letters and papers from over three hundred Corresponding Members and Societies were also read and discussed. Though geography had not yet won the academic status that the Council thought was desirable, marked progress had been made; the Society's examinations revealed a great advance in the standard of teaching in primary schools. The lecture programmes were bringing the subject to the attention of the general public and the *Journal* had made a real contribution to geographical literature whilst the various collections had been built up rapidly and satisfactorily. 'The Manchester Geopraghical Society', Sowerbutts said, 'was founded to raise a note of alarm and to provide the requisite information and concentration of effort to remedy the evil . . . to attract attention to the prime necessities of a commercial nation.' Sowerbutts, in fact, steadily maintained that the fundamental work of the Society lay in the commercial field and that the scientific aspect must follow later.

The year 1899 began with a reception to celebrate the 500th meeting of the Society. Shortly afterwards Herbertson came down from his new post at the Heriot-Watt College in Edinburgh to talk on 'the Teaching of Applied Geography and on the Position of Economic Geography in Education', subjects of considerable interest to members at that time, particularly in view of the anxiety they felt at the lack of progress at Owens College. A. W. Flux lectured there on Political and Commercial Geography, B. Hobson on Geology and Physical Geography, whilst such outstanding men as Tait and Tout helped with the historical approach, Boyd Dawkins with Geology and Palaeontology, Weiss with Botany, Schuster and Core with Physics, an illustrious list, but the subject itself was still regarded as a poor relation, barely recognized. Moreover, Lecturers in Geography were coming and going with monotonous and harmful regularity; Flux had lasted no longer than Herbertson.

On numerous occasions deputations from the Society interviewed Principal Ward in an attempt to improve the status of geography, and eventually this continued harrying began to produce results. When Flux left in 1899, he was succeeded by A. J. Sargent of Brazenose College, Oxford, and before long courses were available as follows: Political and Commercial Geography, (1) Preliminary, two hours per week; (2) Special subject, 1 hour; Physical Geography (under the aegis of Geology) a course of 30 lectures per session included Physiographical Geography and Geomorphology.

The Education Committee also took up the cudgels with the Yorkshire Union over the neglect of the subject in their new scheme, with the result that the Society organized examinations for the Union later in the year with China as the special area. Thus, by continual hammering, the Society kept alive the cause of geography in the local area.

Meanwhile other activities continued on as large a scale as finances would permit. It is interesting to record that S. H. Brooks one of the Trustees, hired the Albion Hotel for an evening lecture on the Scilly Islands illustrated by no less than 400 slides, surely an all-time record. As if this were not enough, 'Geography' announced that 'to add to the further interest of the address, music will be given during the evening. Mr. Brooks offers to the members at the close, a cup of beef tea and sandwiches. Ladies are respectfully requested not to wear their bonnets or hats.' Even this failed to satisfy the members, and later in the year Sowerbutts led a large party to the islands to see for themselves.

Then, arising out of the meeting of the Imperial Institute a meeting was called in Manchester further to discuss the establishment of commercial geographical museums throughout the country. A committee was appointed, with Sowerbutts as secretary, and lists of desirable specimens were prepared. Though most of the provincial societies were represented at this and subsequent meetings, real enthusiasm was absent, and the idea soon died a natural death.

The Rev. S. A. Steinthal attended the International Geographical Congress in Berlin in 1899 on behalf of the Society, and returned deeply lamenting the lack of Government support in Britain as compared with Continent. He had found that every Prussian university had had a Chair of Geography since 1870 whereas Britain had Professors only in London and Cardiff and Readers at Oxford and Cambridge. Apart from these, the only institute for higher education giving the subject any place in its examinations was the Victoria University, and then only because of constant pressure from the Manchester Geographical Society and the personal sympathies of the Principal. Even so, Herbertson had been lost, first to Edinburgh and then to Oxford.

44

Fortunately, however, the occupants of these key positions were men of ability and foresight and the Society was greatly heartened when, in February 1900, H. J. Mackinder visited Manchester bringing with him details of the new School of Geography at Oxford of which he was head and which had been created by the university in co-operation with the Royal Geographical Society. The subject of his lecture to members was 'An Ascent of Mount Kenya' and this was described by the Press as 'a piece of clean and complete geographical work which may be taken as a model for the future'. Geography was clearly beginning to establish itself in Britain even if the going in Manchester was hard.

As the century drew to its close, the Council became more and more aware that the lease of the Parsonage rooms expired in December 1900 and that the problem of finding accommodation had returned after a lapse of barely five years. At the instigation of the Vice-Chairman a committee consisting of the officers, Professor Core, Councillor Hassall and J. H. Reed, was set up to consider the condition of the Society with reference to 'necessary future developments'. The committee soon reached the conclusion that a bigger building was urgently needed to house the Society's numerous possessions, to provide a large lecture hall, a members' room to allow for a commercial museum, and a proper map room. Even at this general stage, Council could see that the task ahead was one of no mean proportions, so they strengthened the Committee with the addition of E. W. Mellor, S. L. Keymer, S. H. Brooks, J. D. L. Wilde, Dentith, John Thomason, W. J. Crossley and N. Kolp. Incidentally, Wilde was Eli Sowerbutts' son-in-law and had been an Hon. Secretary of the Society. He was an Oxford graduate and winner of the Harmsworth Prize for Geography.

One of the first decisions was for increased membership, for it will be remembered that funds had fallen so low that even the *Journal* had to suffer economies, and that this increase should be achieved whilst other planning proceeded so that the inevitable costs could be met. Accordingly Messrs Agar and Newlove were appointed canvassers.

The time, however, passed quickly, and with less than a year to run, no solution had been found, no practical scheme envisaged. Some positive action became essential, and in the end negotiations

45

with the Dean and Chapter of Manchester Cathedral, who owned the site, resulted in a temporary extension of the lease. The position still remained critical even after this concession, and with a view to further urgent steps being taken, F. B. Oppenheim was elected Solicitor to the Society.

In the short breathing space thus gained, discussions went on apace but without any real progress until it was learned that the Dean and Chapter would be prepared to grant a new lease of the land for 999 years at a rent of £237 per annum on condition that the Society erected a new building on the site. This news canalized thought and the Council began to talk of a fine new house that would end all their accommodation difficulties. Equanimity, however, received a sharp jolt when enquiries as to the nature of a building sufficient to satisfy the ground landlords elicited the information that the latter stipulated that the letting value of the new property must be two to three times the amount of the ground rent.

From this reply, it was clear that up to £10,000 would be necessary, a vast sum considering the perpetual poverty of the Society. Already June 1901 had come without any significant increase in resources. An appeal had been suggested in 1900, but the Council had ruled the time inopportune owing to the war in South Africa and the famine in India. The patience of the Dean and Chapter would not last for ever, and something must be done in the near future, so a special committee was charged with the task, the members being Harry Nuttall, J. H. Lewis, B. Oppenheim, J. H. Reed, S. L. Keymer, E. W. Mellor, S. H. Brooks, and T. W. Sowerbutts.

The costs of the new building were based largely on surmise, so the committee decided to obtain a more precise figure by asking a number of firms to submit estimates for a building with five floors and two basements, and providing for a shop on the ground floor. Under this arrangement the Society would, for the present, occupy the two top floors, subletting the remainder until such time as it was required and could be afforded. It was at this stage that it was discovered that there would be difficulties in obtaining immediate possession of the whole site, whereupon the Dean and Chapter agreed that the new building need not be completed until the end of 1905. The Council began to breathe more easily.

Eli Sowerbutts agreed that a special appeal should be made to raise the capital but the majority of the Council held the opinion that the amount needed would never be reached in this way. Instead the suggestion was made that a Manchester Geographical Society Building Company should be floated with shares of £10 each, and that members should be invited to purchase as many as possible. This plan carried the day, and Council asked the Trustees to act on behalf of the Society.

The negotiations with the cathedral authorities and the preliminary arrangements for the new company were all going well when S. H. Brooks resigned from his Trusteeship, being unwilling to enter into the new agreement. This might well have proved a major disaster but fortunately Mellor and Nuttall, both men of substance, stepped into the breach and signed the documents on condition that the company was formed with a minimum of delay as, until it came into being, they personally ran a heavy financial risk, being responsible for the rent, covenants, etc. But for the public spirit of these two men, the whole scheme would have foundered.

Subsequently, there were minor difficulties over a clause in the agreement relating to the handing over of the lease from the Trustees to the company, but on 17 January 1902 all the formalities were completed and the Council asked the Building Company to take action as soon as possible.

With the lease problem looming large on the horizon, and the unsettling conditions brought about by the war in Africa, the Society led a fairly quiet life. The lectures followed much their usual pattern, with a predominance of contributions by members, but distinguished visitors included Professor Patrick Geddes, who spoke about 'Geography at the Paris Exhibition' and Captain Deasy on his travels in Tibet, and Clement Wragge on Australia. The contributions made by members at this period were of good quality and had the advantage that many of them dealt with the local area.

The disturbed conditions did not permit the Education Committee much scope and its members limited themselves to a watching brief. The Council meanwhile considered the difficulties of obtaining accurate up-to-date information from abroad, and Sowerbutts proposed that the Society should appoint special representatives to draw up confidential reports. The annual accounts, however, frustrated his scheme as income persisted in falling short of expenditure and could only be balanced by means of special donations, this at a time when a new building was required. Only the Victorians continued to make headway, delivering sixy-five lectures, including three in France by C. H. Bellamy.

With 1900 conditions gradually improved, and Sowerbutts could gratify his love of the commercial aspect by bringing G. M. Brice to speak on the influence that the new Trans-Siberian Railway would have on trade, and the more academically minded heard G. E. Stromeyer speak on Penck's million map.

Sowerbutts, too, had been quietly working away at his commercial museum, his enthusiasm quite unaffected by the fact that the Society might at any time lose its quarters. Eventually his persistence was rewarded: on 11 March 1901 Harry Nuttall (Vice-Chairman of the Council) formally opened the Commercial and Geographical Museum.

All the same, some anxiety was felt about the health of the Society, and at the Annual Dinner in 1901, J. H. Reed voiced his concern at the large number of members who were content to play a passive role and complained that the lecture audiences were nothing like as large as they should be.

Hampered by lack of money and with his commercial museum now achieved, Eli Sowerbutts turned his energies towards increasing the correspondence with other societies and to exchanging papers with them. We also find him making contacts with the new Southampton Geographical Society of which the Hon. John S. Montague, M.P., was President, and W. H. Rogers Hon. Secretary.

With this correspondence came a letter from Herbertson in which he wrote that Freshfield and he were both envious of Manchester's use of *Geography* as the title of their monthly bulletin, for otherwise the Geographical Association would have used it for their journal instead of *The Geographical Teacher*. In point of fact, after *Geography* ceased to appear in 1905, they did take the name over some years later, and have used it ever since.

At the end of the year J. H. Reed lectured to the children on 'With Roberts to Pretoria' and this occasion is the first on which it is recorded that the cinematograph was used by the Society. In connection with children, the answers in the prize competition

48

showed tangible evidence of the higher standard of teaching in local schools.

During the autumn, when it had become clear that a company would have to be floated to erect a £10,000 building, the Council issued a brochure inviting promises of support for the Building Company. The appeal was based on the grounds that the future of the Society should be safeguarded as it had produced evidence of its worth in the following ways:

(1) It had been instrumental in establishing Geography at Owens College.
(2) It had brought many eminent travellers and explorers to the city.
(3) The Victorian lecture panel had awakened interest in Geography by lecturing to 150,000 in eight years.
(4) It had to some extent offset the nfluence of subsidized foreign Societies of Commercial Geography.

The response was most gratifying, and by the end of 1901 over £3000 had been promised including £500 each from Nuttall, Oppenheim, Thomason and Pilkington, £300 from Kolp and Philips, £250 from Woolley and Sir Bosdin Leech, whilst Joel Wainwright initiated a Furnishing Fund. This start gave the Council heart, and the new home, though still not achieved, had at least become possible.

A crippling lack of funds for ordinary activities, coupled with uncertainties about the new building, made 1902 a difficult year. This is very apparent in the lecture programme for, even with help from members willing to speak on their travels, Eli Sowerbutts himself had to deliver two lectures in the spring to maintain regular weekly meetings. Only rarely could a large hall be afforded, and the only distinguished visitor was L. W. Lyde who spoke on the teaching of geography in schools.

The Victorians continued their triumphant progress. One of their number R. W. Swallow, was appointed a professor at the new university of Tai Yuen Fu, and thereafter the Society received many interesting reports on the conditions and geography of Shansi.

Whilst planning of the new quarters went quietly forward, the Chairman of Council (Rev. S. A. Steinthal) reviewed the state of the Society. He said that he found much that was satisfactory, particularly that by rigid economy the deficit had been reduced. So far as the *Journal* was concerned the quality had been maintained at such a level of excellence that the Royal Geographical Society had even taken it as a model when changing the style of their own publication. Eli Sowerbutts, after twelve trips to the Continent to inspect commercial museums in France, Belgium, and Italy, had, with the energetic support of Casartelli, established the Society's own museum in the face of many difficulties. Continuous pressure on the university had produced encouraging results in the educational field and it was now hoped that a good commercial faculty would soon be established there.

During 1903, the pattern was very similar, recovery being threatened by the deplorable state of the cotton trade as the result of financial speculation in America. The Victorians took this opportunity to offer a lecture on 'Cotton Growing within the British Empire' which drew many requests. The Council received with interest the 'Syllabus of Instruction in Geography' issued by the Royal Geographical Society at the request of the Oxford and Cambridge Schools Examinations Board, and the London School Board. Subject to minor amendments, they approved the document, feeling that here was another solid step forward.

Excursions, which had decreased in numbers over the last few years, still attracted the faithful few. Their geographical content had rather given way to sightseeing, but it is amusing to find one advertised in the programme as a 'Geographical Pleasant Saturday afternoon: The Manager of Salford Corporation Sewage Works invited members'!

The finances were a little easier in 1904 and the programme immediately became more ambitious, it being possible to invite the Rev. Dr. McFarlane again to speak on New Guinea, and W. B. Steveni on 'Travels in Russia'. Herbertson, too, paid another visit on which he gave one of his brilliant talks on the region around Oxford. Then in March Cardwell spoke on the 'Preparation of a Course in Local Geography'. This spring session was to be the last in the old building, and the Council was anxious to strengthen the Society as much as possible before the 12–18 months when it would be without a home.

Then, quite suddenly, the Society received a hard blow. On the

30 April 1904 Eli Sowerbutts died, aged nearly seventy, after a short illness—he had been at his desk only a fortnight previously. By his devoted work, he had carved for himself a special niche in the history of British Geography. As the events previously recorded all testify, the success of the Manchester Geographical Society was almost entirely due to his inspiration and his never-flagging enthusiasm. Though he was not spared to see it in its new home, at least he had the satisfaction of sharing in the planning and of seeing the final plans of Messrs. Sankey and Cubbon approved. Then just before his death the £8500 contract was let to Messrs. Wilson and Toft.

III

The Harry Sowerbutts Era
1905–19

The death of its chief executive officer placed a heavy burden on the honorary officials, all the more so as demolition and rebuilding were imminent. To meet the emergency the Council immediately set up an Executive Committee consisting of the Officers with Messrs Mellor and Philips, and appointed Harry Sowerbutts—Eli's second son and an active member of the Society and of the Victorians for many years—as Assistant Secretary. Fortunately, he could work his accountancy business from the Society's rooms, otherwise the £75 would surely never have attracted him. The Executive Committee, meeting at fortnightly intervals and reporting to very occasional meetings of Council, shouldered the bulk of the administration; the *Journal* and *Geography* were temporarily transferred to the Hon. Secretaries, and soon the latter ceased publication in favour of announcing meetings by postcard.

In spite of this catastrophe, the Society managed to continue in much the same way as before. For the autumn lectures, rooms were variously booked at the Coal Exchange, the Chamber of Commerce and Owens College; for committees, advantage was taken of Harry Sowerbutt's office at the Coal Exchange and for the storage of the Library, Museum, etc., the Executive Committee rented a house at 85 Shakespeare Street, Chorlton-on-Medlock. The Victorians, though deprived of their chairman, operated from the Coal Exchange with unaltered efficiency.

The lectures themselves followed much the same pattern with a few outside speakers and rather more from amongst the members, but in November 1904 the Society welcomed Captain Scott to the Free Trade Hall to speak on the 'Farthest South', the national Antarctic expedition. The event proved to be highly successful and, as Scott said at the time 'in no other town have I received such a warm welcome and been so magnificently treated as in Manchester'.

At Owens College, now the Victoria University of Manchester, yet another change in the geographical lectureship had come about with the arrival of John Macfarlane, a man of far higher calibre than either Flux or Sargent, so that the Council felt that progress was in the right direction though still lamentable slow. Geography in the Government service however, was not so healthy and in October the Council felt it necessary to send the following resolution to seven Government departments, a step that led to protracted correspondence in the national press.

In future, in all examinations that are held in the several departments of the Government for entrance to the public service, Geography should be treated as an independent subject and a separate paper or papers should be set in it and a substantial proportion of marks should be assigned to it in the regulations.

The lack of premises and the emergency administration made for unsettled conditions, and in consequence lecture audiences declined, even though the Spring Syllabus 1905 contained some excellent talks like that by Woolley on climbing in the Canadian Rockies. To make matters worse, losses by death were exceptionally high and included H. M. Steinthal. The Victorians, however, did their best to maintain interest and organized a meeting at the Whitworth Institute where papers were read on Geography in Schools, in Business, and in Pleasure. Giving the first, H. C. Martin reported that in spite of recent advances, there remained much scope for improvement, above all for textbooks which appealed to logic and reason; the encouragement of local observational geography was a fundamental requirement.

As that summer of 1905 progressed, and the building began to take shape, the Council turned their thoughts towards the choice of some suitable person to perform the opening ceremony. The President was the natural first suggestion, but the Prince of Wales declined as he was on the point of leaving for India. The Dukes of Devonshire and Argyll and the President of the Royal Geographical Society were also unable to accept, whereupon it was decided that the opening ceremony should be performed by Sir Thomas Shann, the Lord Mayor.

The new building, overlooking the quiet lawns of the Parsonage Gardens, and yet only a short walk from busy Deansgate, had been designed in a simple, but dignified, style. The front elevation consisted of red pressed bricks relieved by terra-cotta; all the staircases and corridors were of fireproof construction; and the amenities included electric light and a hydraulic passenger lift. The long-felt want for a Members' Room, a Library and a Map Room had also been answered, and the Society would now possess a fine Lecture Hall seating over two hundred persons and equipped with a splendid lantern presented by E. W. Mellor.

The official opening took place on Thursday 19 October 1905, a date corresponding with the 21st anniversary of the foundation. The Lord Mayor was received in the entrance hall by members of the Building Company and then conducted to the Members' Room to be welcomed by the Rev. S. A. Steinthal and the Council. For the ceremonial opening, the Chairman led him to the door of the Lecture Hall, there presenting him with an ornamental tray.

In the proceedings that followed, the Lord Mayor was supported on the platform by the Rev. S. A. Steinthal (Chairman of Council), Colonel G. E. Church (Royal Geographical Society), Alfred Hopkinson (Vice-Chancellor of Manchester University), Harry Nuttall (President of the Chamber of Commerce) and Dr. J. L. Paton (High Master of Manchester Grammar School), whilst among the audience were representatives from other societies in Manchester and many distinguished guests. Speeches gave way to refreshments, and these, in turn, to an evening of lantern slides and music.

The *Courier* describing the occasion wrote: 'The Society has ever placed the educational side of its existence on the same level of importance as the exploratory; its work has been quiet and unobtrusive, yet influential.'

Though the new premises offered great opportunities for expanding the work and influence of the Society, and though the autumn lectures included such topics as 'Younghusband's Mission to Lhasa' by Major C. H. D. Ryder, d.s.o., 'Through Yunnan to Tonquin' by Mrs. Archibald Little, and 'Weather Forecasting' by William Marriott, f.r.met.s., the effort necessary to raise so much capital had sorely taxed its finances. At the end of the year there were forty outstanding subscriptions in a membership of 565, and an appeal for £600 to clear existing commitments realized only £341 and the gift of some furniture for the Members' Room from J. J. Gleave.

Even though shackled financially, Council maintained the standard of the lectures in 1906, and as their attractiveness drew increasing audiences, hearts were high. The call on the Victorians fell to a mere sixteen lectures that winter, half of them given by J. H. Reed, but their enthusiasm never faltered, and they increased the slide collection until it contained over five thousand items.

The social aspect, which had always formed such a strong feature of the Society's activities, continued to flourish. The Children's Party early in January, with its entertainments and awarding of prizes for those who had excelled in the little examinations organized by the Council, was highly successful. So, too, was the Annual Dinner in June, which Lord Stanley of Alderley attended as chief guest. This team spirit, however, found its highest expression in November in the presentation of an illuminated address to S. A. Steinthal to mark his 80th birthday, and of a silver rose bowl to J. H. Reed on the occasion of his silver wedding as a practical token of gratitude. This sense of corporate activity also led to a revival of local excursions—to Melandra, Marple, Great Hucklow, etc.—though members were slow to make suggestions.

The encouragement of geographical education had been a prime interest from the outset, and N. Kolp now anonymously established a prize to be awarded in the name of the Society on the results of the geography examinations at the university. How appropriate his gesture was may be seen from a letter written to the Secretary by J. MacFarlane: 'I have just finished examining 240 matriculation candidates in Geography and I cannot but feel how much has still to be done before we can congratulate ourselves that the subject is properly taught.' Later in the year, this trained and missionary spirited geographer had an opportunity to fight for his beliefs for he came to strengthen the Executive Committee.

The Society has always displayed the ability to foresee the potentialities of men before public recognition of this distinction. The invitation to Sven Hedin was a case in point, and another was the bringing to Manchester in February 1907 of F. J. Russell (later Sir John Russell), then of Wye Agricultural College, to talk about the 'Relation between Geographical Position and the Productive Capacity of Land'. This, and a lecture by Hilaire Belloc on 'The Influence of Physical Geography on the Destiny of Nations' evince proof of the wide view held by Council on the scope of geographical studies. Strangely, however, the same syllabus advertised a lecture on 'The Formation of Glaciers, with Views taken on Glaciers and round Mount Vesuvius'. For a meeting when the Hon. J. H. Rason spoke on 'Western Australia, its Possibilities and Prospects', the Society joined forces with the Chamber of Commerce and the Ship Canal Company.

Travel and exploration received due attention, an outstanding lecture being on 'The Kut Desert' by H. R. Sykes, m.a., and 'Through Unknown Labrador' by Mrs. Leonidas Hubbard.

Nearer home, Dr. E. M. Wrench described 'The Effects of Glaciers in the Derwent Valley, Derbyshire', and local excursions took members into the field to see for themselves.

During the autumn of 1906 the Extension Committee sent out circulars in an effort to increase membership, but only twelve nominations were received, with the result that the year-end revealed a deficit of £120. The new year brought larger audiences, the 220 at the lecture on 12 March being the highest number for a long time, but economies had to be made and the younger assistant, H. Goulburn, was replaced by an office boy. Even the *Journal* was put out to competitive tender. This stringency seemed to affect the Society's morale, for only twenty attended the Annual Dinner to hear a strenuous appeal for an increased membership, if only on the grounds that Manchester men had made their money and expanded their businesses from the results of exploration. The prospects at this time looked bleak indeed, but had the future been visible, those present would have been more content. As it was, July brought the sad news of the death of Monsignor Gadd, a devoted supporter, and of the failing health of S. A. Steinthal, who was virtually confined to his study, though still keenly interested in the Society and its doings.

On the educational side Macfarlane was able to report that as a result of sustained representation, the Civil Service Commissioners had agreed to include geography in their examinations, probably from 1909. By the end of 1907 prospects had visibly improved. Both membership and attendances at meetings had shown substantial improvements, and the accounts showed that the deficit stood at only £162.

The spring lecture session for 1908 turned out to be still more heartening. The lectures, preponderantly on Eastern Europe and volcanoes, drew much larger audiences, with the result that the

Executive Committee asked the Building Company in March to consider putting a gallery in the Hall. The *Journal*, too, was healthy and such was the harmonious co-operation with the Royal Geographical Society that increasing use of the latter's maps was made to illustrate articles.

Shortly afterwards, in June, the Society was happy to receive a party of twenty members from the Commercial Geographical Society of Paris led by M. Paul Labbé, the secretary. In London for the Franco-British Exhibition, they had expressed a desire to see something of the North of England. After a formal lunch they were conducted on a short tour of the sights, including the Royal Exchange, a spinning mill, and the docks. This was followed by an informal meeting with members and a dinner at the Midland Hotel, where the Manchester officers strove to further cement the 'Entente Cordiale' with speeches in French.

Into the blue summer sky, however, drifted two clouds. The first was the death of Mrs. Rylands. Apart from the loss of a useful member, there was the problem of her shares which came on the market. The Society had no funds to buy them, but rather than let the opportunity pass, several members offered to become Life Members to make the purchase possible. Later in the year similar gestures by other members enabled the Society to acquire the shares belonging to J. D. Wilde, whilst Steinthal and Kolp transferred their own holdings as gifts. Thus began the gradual process of gathering in all the shares which has continued up to the present.

The other cloud could not be dissipated so easily. With his advancing age and his continued inability to attend meetings, S. A. Steinthal felt obliged to resign as Chairman of Council. Such was his attachment to the Society and his belief in its purpose that he offered to continue as Editor, for this was a task he could perform without leaving his study. As he himself put it in a letter to J. H. Reed, 'I think everyone who has taken any active part in the work of the Society has not only derived intellectual advantage from his connections, but has valued the genial spirit and sympathy which has bound him so delightfully to a companionship with kindred minds, and added many happy hours to his life.'

Steinthal's resignation entailed some re-organization. Harry Nuttall, who had been largely responsible for the new building and was now an M.P., agreed to become Chairman, and after twenty-four years of loyal service as one of the Hon. Secretaries, Fritz Zimmern succeeded to the Vice-Chairmanship.

This same summer saw the Geographical Association establish a Manchester branch. Very appropriately Herbertson came up from Oxford to deliver the inaugural address on 'Some Educational Aspects of Geography'. Equally appropriately, the meeting on 19 May took place in the Parsonage, and for subsequent meetings the Association used the Members' Room on Saturday mornings. About this time, too, it was reported that the Scottish Geographical Society had 1950 members, the Liverpool Society 588, and the membership of the Manchester Geographical Society was 641. Leeds also had a society of its own. The star of geography was in the ascendant.

Good progress could also be reported in the educational field. At the Annual Meeting it became clear that the Vice-Chancellor of the university was an ally. Indeed, Hopkinson admitted to a little fanaticism in favour of geography.

As the Society entered its 25th year in 1909, prospects seemed better than ever. True, finances were exiguous, but at last annual accounts were beginning to balance. Further, several members, like Henry Kirkpatrick, had answered the Council's appeal to those who held shares in the Building Company to either donate or bequeath them to the Society. Steinthal and a few others made special gifts to cover the visits of several expensive lectures. Thus emboldened, the Council promoted Harry Sowerbutts to the Secretaryship at a princely £100 p.a., and even Arthur Marshman, the librarian, could have his wages raised from 21s. to 22s. per week at the age of twenty-three.

The lecture programme maintained a high standard and saw the beginning of the Society's warm and fruitful association with that outstanding personality, Bishop Welldon, with a talk on 'Thoughts on Travel over the Empire'. Perhaps the greatest interest in the spring of 1909, though, centred on a return visit from Sven Hedin, now a popular hero, to talk about 'Through Unknown Tibet'. For this special occasion, the Free Trade Hall was taken, and with every seat sold, the Society made a welcome £130 profit. Next day the university received the explorer amidst scenes of great jubilation, and the visit reached its climax with the Society's banquet in his honour.

Encouraged by this success, the Council arranged to take the Free Trade Hall again in the autumn for a lecture by E. H. Shackleton on 'Nearest the South Pole' followed, next day, by a banquet at the Midland Hotel, with Shackleton as guest of honour, to mark the 25th anniversary of the Society. In a speech to the assembled 240 members and friends, Bishop Casartelli told how

> The Society's aims from the very beginning . . . were of a somewhat more practical nature than was at all possible with a great scientific society like the Royal Geographical Society. It is true our aim has always been, and always ought to be, the promotion of geographical science as a science, but it was not limited to that in the minds of those who gathered round in the first early days. Its aims were essentially practical, to benefit the community in which we live by making Geography subserve not only the expansion of science, but also the needs and wants of the immense industrial community in which we live. It was to be primarily a Commercial Geographical Society. I know that was the idea in the mind of Dr. Vaughan and of those associated with him, that a Society like this ough to help the trade and industry of this great community and country by making better known those various markets throughout the world which we at present need.

It was in connection with these festivities that Messrs. Lafayette prepared the large diagram, with photographs of nearly all the members arranged in a concentric pattern, which now hangs in the Secretary's office.

Other incidents in this period include the delivery by the indefatigable J. H. Reed of the Inaugural Address of the Kingston-on-Hull Geographical Society. Then as an outcome of the visit by the Paris Commercial Geographical Society in 1908, the Society had the pleasure of hearing Mademoiselle Gabriela de Bolivar, who had been one of the party, speak on 'Venezuela'. The same year also brought the first of several lectures over the next decade by Miss Edna Walter, H.M.I.

The principal event of 1910 concerned the Presidency, for on the death of Edward VII, the Prince of Wales became George V. The Society approached the Home Office to discover what the effect would be on the Presidency, and at the same time enquiring as to the possibility of a Charter and the prefix 'Royal'. The Under Secretary of State declined to recommend the Charter, but in August the Society heard that the king would be graciously pleased to become Patron. Ever since this time, the Society has been privileged with this honour from the reigning monarch.

There now existed a vacancy for a President, and after lengthy discussion, the Council decided that in future the office should be held by an active member instead of some local celebrity as a figurehead. Thus began a line of domestic Presidents, all of whom have been intimately connected with the day-to-day activities of the Society. The choice of the first such office-bearer fell naturally on Harry Nuttall, and members were happy to elect him in recognition of his long and devoted service to the Society. He held this office for the next ten years, and though he rarely attended the formal meetings of committees, he kept in close touch with developments and gave every help within his power.

By sad coincidence, on the very day that Edward VII died, the Society suffered another grievous loss in the death of the Rev. S. A. Steinthal, who, with Eli Sowerbutts, had done so very much in shaping the destinies and formulating the character of the Manchester Geographical Society. Aged 84, he had been in failing health for some months, but though he had withdrawn from active participation, his interest never flagged and he was correcting proofs of the *Journal* to within a week of his death. Shortly afterwards followed the loss of Professor T. H. Core, a sterling member of the Education Sub-Committee.

Outstanding lectures included visits by R. F. Peary to the Free Trade Hall to speak on 'How I reached the Pole' and Aural Stein to a joint meeting with the university on 'Explorations in Central Asia 1906–8'. The less spectacular lectures, however, drew audiences averaging about 300, and included such speakers as Mrs. Arthur Schuster on 'Through Ladakh and Lahore', Dr. Tempest Anderson on 'Volcanoes of Matauena, Samoa' and Sir Bosdin Leech on 'The Panama Canal'.

Members themselves were active in the geographical field. In January 1911 Herbertson was promoted Professor at Oxford, and later in the year, President of Section E of the British Association, his address being 'Geography and Some of its Present Needs'. It is of interest to find him writing to Harry Sowerbutts 'I owe so much [to the M.G.S.] for I began my official career as a geographical lecturer at Owens College, and profited much by the wisdom of Eli Sowerbutts as well as by the maps and books of the Society.' J. H. Reed too spoke to the British Association on 'Cotton Growing within the British Empire', a lecture repeated before the Royal Geographical Society and the Royal Scottish Geographical Society early the following year.

The year 1911 was one of quiet consolidation. Though no outstandingly eminent lecturers came, the lectures provided had a considerable scientific value. For example, Dr. A. Wilmore dealt with 'Some Geographical Problems of the Mid Pennines', Sir Thomas Holland with 'The Systematic Study of a Great Earthquake'—Kangre, 4 April 1904', and Dr. C. E. Moss with 'A Botanical Visit to the Algerian Sahara'. J. B. Charcot however attracted only a poor audience for his lecture on 'The Second French Antarctic Expedition 1908'. During the autumn, Mellor again arranged three open lectures in the Y.M.C.A. Hall which attracted up to 800 people.

Though the financial position had eased, when Egbert Steinthal became Editor, he found that funds would suffice only for a small *Journal*. Though it still continued to appear in quarterly parts, the number of pages was fewer, and the following year summaries began to replace lectures *in extenso*.

The achievements of Scott's Antarctic Expedition aroused considerable interest in Manchester not only on account of the attempt to be first at the South Pole, but also because Scott was a personal friend of Fritz Zimmern, and Ponting, the official cameraman, belonged to the district. Thus news of the tragic failure came as a severe shock. The officers reacted quickly, asking the Lord Mayor to open a fund to help the dependants of those who had died. It so happened that a new 'Electric Theatre' was about to open in Oxford Street, and Council persuaded the proprietors to show the first lot of films received from the expedition and to devote the first two days' takings to the Fund. Mrs. Scott made a special journey from London for the opening, and W. Clarke, Mellor, Oppenheim and Reed addressed the audiences before each showing. In this way, about £145 was raised, together with £180 by public subscription.

Human aspects of geography came to the forefront in the lectures of 1912 with R. W. Williamson on 'The Mafalu People of British New Guinea', Rev. A. S. Rogers 'Life amongst the Hottentots and Bushmen', Dr. Eric Marshall 'Amongst the Pygmies of Dutch New Guinea', and at a joint meeting with the university, Walter McClintock on 'My Life amongst the Indians'. Only at the end of the year did the polar regions figure again in the programme when Roald Amundsen told a packed audience 'How We Reached the South Pole'. During the autumn Mellor, who seems to have assumed the role of beneficent dictator, again provided three open lectures in the Society's name in the Houldsworth Hall, with audiences of 900 or more.

The Victorians, who had been delivering lectures throughout the district, and quietly encouraging the social side of the Society (as well as helping its finances) with whist drives, organized a special Children's Fancy Dress Dance at which costumes had to represent different countries. They also contemplated forming a Touring Club, though the project fell through.

Finance continued to be a stumbling block—even a telephone costing £6 per annum could not be afforded—though the situation improved slightly later in the year when R. G. Lawson and F. B. Oppenheim successfully established the right of the Society to reclaim income tax on its investments as a charity. The staff in these more spacious days included the Secretary (Sowerbutts), the Librarian (Marshman) and a succession of office boys. The library in fact was growing so fast that additional shelving had to be installed and a new index compiled.

The Council continued to press wherever possible for a better status for geography, and it was with gratification that McFarlane could report that the subject's position in degree examinations had greatly improved. Even within the Society itself, a desire for higher standards emerged, leading to the suggestion to form a small study section on the lines of the old library meetings. Kalisch, to whom the project was very dear, agreed to draft the circulars. To end the year 1912, the Society arranged an exhibition in the main hall of some 500 photographs of West Central Africa by the Rev. J. H. and Mrs. Harris.

By 1913 the Society's activities had settled down into a regular pattern with a fairly steady membership about 650. The financial position too was becoming clearer, even if it meant restricting activities to what could be afforded. Towards the end of 1913, the Building Company could pay no dividends on its shares owing to part of the building being unlet, but the position was no longer desperate especially as the Treasurer managed to collect a large number of outstanding subscriptions.

The Scott Fund remained open until March 1913, and Council felt justified in issuing a last appeal to members which realized £140 and brought the Manchester Fund to £1630.

To celebrate the Livingstone centenary, Sir Harry Johnston addressed a meeting in the Albert Hall attended by nearly a thousand members and friends, on 'Livingstone's Explorations and their results'. Afterwards the Society organized a banquet. The other notability in the programme, Commander E. R. G. R. Evans, lectured in the Free Trade Hall in October on the 'British Antarctic Expedition 1910–13'.

In the educational field, Council gave consideration to the establishment of a scholarship in geography at the university, but they had to defer action owing to the tightness of finances. The following year the late B. Oppenheim's bequest of ten £10 shares reached the Society, and George Thomas gave a similar amount, but even then Council decided that it would be unwise to proceed.

The spring before the outbreak of the war found the audiences so large that serious consideration had to be given to limiting admissions. When the war broke out in 1914, the Executive Committee suggested suspending lectures, but Council would not agree on the grounds that they would afford some measure of relief from the horrors of war. As Bishop Welldon pointed out at the time, there would be such political and material changes when the war was over as had seldom occurred in past history, and it was most important to increase our knowledge of geography. The international tension and the news items streaming in from all parts of the world engendered a greatly increased interest in other lands, and the large audiences of the spring grew larger still, and on several occasions in the autumn, not only was the Hall packed, with as many as sixty standing, but many had to be turned away. This situation had to be met by holding lectures a second time. These lectures dealt largely with the parts of Europe involved in the fighting, and in December the threads were drawn together when Hilaire Belloc spoke in the Free Trade Hall on 'The Strategy of the War'.

Owing to the international situation, activity other than lectures was almost at a standstill. Rather sadly, at the Annual Meeting in May 1914, J. H. Reed resigned his position as Hon. Secretary after many years of distinguished service, owing to frequent necessary absences from Manchester. He still maintained a close interest though in what was going on. Then a letter of 17 July 1914 from George Thomas, led to the setting up of a Corporate Membership which replaced and broadened the old 'Affiliated Membership' by granting such bodies two transferable admission tickets. That greater use has not been made of this facility by local organizations in the succeeding years is a curiosity of local geographical interest. The university also chose 1914 to institute a Diploma in Geography, an award for which there has been little demand.

The second year of the war brought few changes. Audiences continued large, and the financial position was greatly eased by a gift of £500 from Mrs. Thomason. The *Journal* however had to be reduced to a single volume owing to wartime restrictions. The thousandth ordinary meeting took place in the Houldsworth Hall on 30 November without any special celebrations, most untypical of the Society. It is noteworthy, though, that of the original Council of 1885 five members were still active—Rev. J. C. Casartelli, Sir William Mather, Sir W. H. Houldsworth, Professor Boyd Dawkins and Fritz Zimmern.

A curtailed British Association met in Manchester in early September at which the President of Section E, Major H. G. Lyons, D.SC., F.R.S., called for more analytical and less descriptive geography, a plea which so far as the M.G.S. was concerned, fell on rather deaf ears.

Over the next two years, audiences began to thin out a little until in the autumn of 1917 it was reported that they were the smallest since the gallery was added in 1908. For the convenience of members travelling from a distance, Council instituted afternoon lectures which proved successful.

With so many people on active service, arranging lectures proved difficult. Thus it is interesting to find names such as J. Scott Kettie, Bishop Hanlon, Professor G. Elliott Smith and P. M. Roxby amongst the speakers. The syllabus also included several members who were to become prominent in later years such as T. A. Edwards and Miss K. Qualtrough.

J. H. Reed died in May 1916, the Society losing one of its best and most loyal members. Shortly afterwards news came of the death of Eli Sowerbutts' widow, thus severing another link with the past. To perpetuate the memory of the Sowerbutts, a few of their friends presented £150 to provide an Eli and Emma Sowerbutts Memorial and to enable the tablet to be put on the wall of the Lecture Hall as a permanent record of their gratitude.

The Society also took a deep interest in the proposal of the Manchester Libraries' Committee to set up a Commercial Library, and appointed the President as their representative. The success of this scheme is evident to all those who know the splendid department in the Central Library which has justified itself many times over.

In the spring of 1918, the Geographical Association held its first national meeting outside London, choosing Zeppelin-free Manchester and using the quarters freely offered by the Manchester Geographical Society. The public meetings were held jointly, and for the first Bishop Welldon took the chair, as he represented both bodies, the Geographical Association as President of the Manchester Branch, the Manchester Geographical Society as a Vice-President. When H. J. Fleure addressed the joint audience on 'Regional Survey', he can little have thought that within twelve years the Manchester Geographical Society was to be able to bring him back to Manchester as the first Professor of Geography at the university.

At the annual meeting, Egbert Steinthal retired from the Honorary Secretaryship, being succeeded by T. W. F. Parkinson. This change brought with it a renewed interest in the educational aspects of geography. For some time Nuttall, Parkinson and a few others had been hammering away at this subject with the object of putting geography in such a position in secondary schools that it would enable men to obtain geographical appointments, and thus lead to a demand for more teachers who aspired for higher positions in universities. Nuttall claimed that if a Chair or a course of special studies in geography could be established in the university, it would make possible a spreading all over the country of more efficient teachers. Unless the subject became more prominent in secondary schools, people would not give attention to it, and teachers and others who aspired to higher ranks in the educational field would not take it up.

Manchester, as the Lord Mayor said at the Annual Meeting, had been attempting to put Geography on a higher plane, but with little encouragement from the Board of Education.

Though the Royal Geographical Society was prepared to accept the position and let the Minister of Education have his way, the Manchester Geographical Society was manifestly unhappy. They felt that the policy of the Royal Geographical Society showed that the latter did not realize the serious position in which teachers of Geography in Secondary Schools were placed. Accordingly they persuaded the Chamber of Commerce to protest to the Minister, and wrote to the Royal Geographical Society asking them to give serious consideration to the desirability of getting Geography specifically mentioned as an advanced course subject in the Regulations, a course to which the Royal Geographical Society eventually agreed. Meanwhile members in Manchester lobbied their M.P.s and sent a delegation including Sir Thomas Shann and Spurley Hey to interview Fisher and members of his staff at the Board of Education with regard to the inclusion of geography in special courses for which grants were made. London however proved unhelpful. The attitude of the Society is summed up in the resolution 'That the Manchester Geographical Society deplores the continued omission of Geography from the subjects of study specified in connection with the advanced courses for Secondary Schools and reaffirms its strong conviction that this omission is prejudicial to the general future of Education in this country'. In the meantime, Miss Qualtrough suggested that the Hall should be made available during the day for lectures to school children at which the resources of the museum and slide collection could be used.

At the Annual Meeting in 1918, the usual deficit appeared in the accounts, the total liability being £166. In answer to an appeal to clear this and so permit a fresh start after the war, a number of supporters raised £120, which considerably improved matters, though not providing sufficient for overdue redecorating.

Audiences had settled down to about 230 each week, which the Council considered satisfactory in the circumstances, and 1918 ended with a special display of maps to illustrate a paper by Colonel Crook on 'British Geography during the War'.

IV

The T W Sowerbutts Era
1919-33

With the end of the war, the Society began to look forward to a new era of prosperity and usefulness. It had proved strong enough to survive four years of hostilities, and the finances, though meagre, were sufficient. Such optimism, however, soon suffered a setback with the death in February 1919 of Harry Sowerbutts, the well-loved secretary who had worked with might and main for the welfare of the Society and who had successfully followed in his father's footsteps. Fortunately, however, his elder brother, T. W. Sowerbutts, agreed to take over the position, thus maintaining the family connection which had given so much to Manchester geography.

More changes followed in the summer. Egbert Steinthal assumed responsibility for the *Journal*, and Richard Kay, F.R.G.S. (who had changed his name from Kalisch in 1915), and T. W. F. Parkinson, M.SC., F.G.S., succeeded to the Honorary Secretaryships. When Thomas Gregory retired as Hon. Auditor after thirty-four years' service in favour of John Thomason, F.C.A., another link with the past had been severed. Even then, changes were incomplete, for on 5 June 1919, Fritz Zimmern died, and with the passing of its Chairman of Council, the Society had lost an indefatigable worker who had advanced its cause with complete unostentation. Then Bishop Welldon left the city for Durham, John McFarlane resigned from Council, and Harry Nuttall intimated his desire to resign from the Presidency on moving to the south. He eventually left in December.

Thus it was against a background of fundamental and far-reaching change in personnel that the Society prepared itself for the post-war years. Fortunately, the rank and file remained steadfast and evening audiences continued to exceed two hundred and the monthly Friday afternoon lectures a hundred or more.

Parkinson, a gifted and enthusiastic teacher at the Central High School for Boys, and for many years Chairman of the Manchester Branch of the Geographical Association, began in 1919 to lead the Society in its struggle with the education authorities.

When the Board of Education wrote that there were not sufficient specialists to warrant advanced courses in geography in secondary schools, his immediate reaction was that never had there been a time when geography was so necessary, and at the invitation of the British Association Corresponding Societies' Committee, he drew up a paper setting out his views. In the event, he could not attend the meeting, so T. W. Sowerbutts read it for him. Entitled 'Geography in the Curriculum of Higher Education', it called for much more geography in schools and universities, for more geographers in the Government services, and for the creation of more scholarships and Chairs in geography. In presenting Parkinson's paper, Sowerbutts announced that the Geographical Association was behind the Manchester suggestion that the Minister of Education should be urged to set up a Departmental Committee on Geography similar to that on History. These views found considerable support, from Professors Myres and Peake in particular, and the Association duly passed a resolution on these lines.

The new vitality amongst the leaders of the Society was soon reflected amongst the members, and evening audiences increased to an average of 290 though the Friday afternoon lectures declined in popularity. The Society's collections were strengthened at this time by the gift of all the military maps published during the war, whilst the slide collection had assumed such proportions that it had to be moved from the Enquiry Office into the Museum upstairs, which incidentally began the decline of the Museum.

The winter of 1919 produced further evidence that the Society's activities were well founded for it brought such lecturers as Roxby on China, Fawcett on 'Some Geographical Factors in the evolution of Navigation' and A. G. Ogilvie, then of the Manchester University on 'Glaciers and Ice Sheets'. In March 1919 Council arranged an exhibition in the Hall of over two hundred water-colour drawings of 'Life in China' by Bertha Glazier (Mrs. Frost). Over two thousand people came to see them, special parties of school children being arranged, and members of the Victorians' panel acting as guides.

The Annual Meeting in May 1920 could report that most of the ground lost during the war had been regained, and that representations made to the Board of Education had achieved a fair measure of success as that body had admitted the Society's contentions in principle, even if they did claim the time to be inopportune for any positive action.

The vacancy left by the retirement of Harry Nuttall was filled by the well-merited election of Mellor to the Presidency.

At the same time, the rules were amended to make the offices of President and Chairman of Council an annual appointment subject to a maximum of three years. No steps however were taken to apply this principle to members of the Council. Past Presidents were given a status of their own which entitled them to be *ex officio* members of Council, a wise move which gave the Society the benefit of their experiences and wisdom as elder brethren.

The financial position remained depressing, and with no sign of any better prospects, it was agreed to increase ordinary membership from 21*s.* per annum to 30*s.* and associate membership from 10*s.* 6*d.* to 15*s.* per annum, at which figures they remained until 1949. To attract students and younger members, a new student membership (for under 21) was created. The new rates seem to have had no ill effects, the membership showing only a small decline, and audiences increasing to over 300 in the evenings and 130 in the afternoons.

Whilst the lectures, many on wartime reminiscences, brought a crowded Hall week after week, the Council was deeply concerned with matters educational, viewing with particular concern the serious position into which the teaching of geography at the university had lapsed when Ogilvie left to take up research with the American Geographical Society. In the autumn they passed the resolution

> 'That this meeting views with alarm the very inadequate and decreasing provision for geographical instruction in the University of Manchester, which is the more remarkable when contrasted with the advances made in other educational centres, many of less importance commercially; feeling that Manchester should stand in the front rank as a centre of geographical education and research, resolves to support . . . any measures taken to arouse public interest in an effort to remove what is a reproach to a civilized and progressive community'.

As a result of these strictures, Professor Weiss attended the Council on 24 November 1921 to explain what was being done at the university. His defence obviously allayed their worst fears and convinced the members that good was being done under great difficulties. Nevertheless, they held fast to their contention that Manchester, with its commercial activities extending to all parts of the world, could not be said to be in a satisfactory position until the university was placed in such a financial condition as to be enabled to establish a Chair and School of Geography equal if not superior to any in the country. Council decided to refer the matter to the Education Committee with an instruction to take such steps, in co-operation with the university authorities, as might be required to bring the whole question forcibly before the notice of the community so that, at the proper time, a sufficient fund might be raised to take away any excuse on financial grounds for the neglect of this important subject.

Unfortunately for their aspirations, finances continued to be a source of worry. An appeal for donations during the year raised £188 for a fund in memory of the late Secretary and £130 towards the accumulated deficiency, but the annual acounts, even so, revealed a deficit of £158. In consequence Volumes 37 and 38 of the *Journal* had to be published together as a double volume. Fortunately Colonel Greg gave the Society £200 in 5 per cent Debentures of the Building Company.

Something of the enthusiasm of the old days returned, and the Society prepared an exhibit at the British Association at Cardiff to show the work and activities it undertook.

By the summer of 1922 close collaboration with the university and support from R. N. Rudmose Brown led to the appointment of Professor W. H. Barker of Southampton as Reader in Geography at the University, which gave the Society great pleasure for they well realized how tight the university's finances must be. The Council, in fact, was so appreciative that ways and means of raising an endowment fund to provide or at least help to support a Chair of Geography were carefully discussed.

In other spheres, too, progress continued to be satisfactory. By careful budgeting, and by gifts, the Society had become owners of 40 per cent of the shares in the Building Company; membership had fallen no further; the collections were still growing, the lantern-slides alone numbering over 14,000; the Victorians, though delivering less outside lectures, were playing an important part in maintaining the social side with whist drives and similar activities.

The afternoon lectures, however, attracted so few members that the Council withdrew them at the end of 1922.

Now that the financial outlook had become rather easier, Little decided that it would be a good opportunity for him to resign from the Treasurership which he had held through twenty difficult years. The suggestion met with such opposition, and gave rise to such protestations of regret, that he eventually agreed to carry on—finally resigning in 1925.

Shortly after his arrival, Barker was elected to the Council where his great enthusiasm began to make itself apparent. As early as November he delivered his first lecture on 'The Gold Coast Colony' and before long the lecture programme began to swing towards geography proper and away from travelogues.

Progress in education continued satisfactorily. In October the Board of Education's new syllabus announced that geography might be taken as a special subject, and the university intimated that, despite some opposition in the Senate, there would, in all probability, be an Honours School in Geography in the Faculty of Arts from October 1923. Thus encouraged, plans for endowing the Chair went ahead rapidly, and Mellor, to give practical evidence of his beliefs, inaugurated a Chair of Geography Fund with £1000.

To mark the establishment, at long last, of the Honours School, Barker persuaded the university and the Society to hold a joint exhibition in the Whitworth Hall during January 1923. The theme was 'Maps' and it consisted largely of facsimiles and reproductions of manuscript maps, early printed and modern Ordnance Survey maps, globes, etc., taken mainly from the university's rich Mills and Barker collections. The opening ceremony was performed by Lord Lugard with E. Fiddes, the Senior Pro-Vice-Chancellor, in the Chair.

During the week it was open, a series of experts gave public lectures on maps as follows: Sir George Fordham, 'The Evolution of Maps of the British Isles'; M. C. Andrews, 'Mediaeval Mappae Mondi'; C. S. S. Higham, 'Age of Discovery Maps'; Colonel H. T. Crook, 'Ordnance Survey Maps'; W. H. Barker, 'Early Maps of London'.

The exhibition achieved great success, and in the short time it was open about five thousand people visited it. Favourable Press notices which drew attention to the long and difficult struggle to establish geography on an academic level in Manchester, gave publicity to the endowment fund, and with this support over £1500 had been collected by the autumn.

This new Honours Course consisted in the first year of general introductory studies, in the second year of a more detailed study of three major regions, and in the third year of regional work on France, geographical problems and the history of geographical discovery. Having once favoured geography, the Senate went still further and included the subject in the Final B.Sc. and Ordinary Degree and also accepted it in the Entrance Examinations.

Meanwhile the Society's routine activities prospered. The Hall was full on numerous lecture evenings; the Victorians, by organizing a social evening, raised sufficient funds for the Society to purchase the collection of 1000 slides owned by the late J. J. Cardwell; more shares in the Building Company were bought, and the Council, at the request of the Manchester Branch of the Geographical Association, agreed to allot space in the Members' Room for a permanent exhibition of geography textbooks for use by teachers in the district.

The Annual Meeting for 1923 brought to a close Mellor's Presidency, a period of three years full of solid achievement. With the *Journal* containing articles of outstanding local importance, with success in the educational field, with well-attended lectures, the Society had attained an important peak in its development. Moreover, in electing Colonel H. T. Crook as the new President, members could feel that the direction of the Society had again passed into good hands.

This same year Richard Kay resigned as one of the Hon. Secretaries, to be replaced by W. H. Barker who, though a newcomer, had, with his enthusiasm and ability, made an indelible impression on geographical activities in the city.

Very shortly afterwards Barker's influence becomes clearly visible with the introduction of trained geographers into the lecture syllabus. For many years the Society had fought for a proper Department of Geography at the university and now they were beginning to receive the benefits of their success. Thus, from 1924 onwards we find names such as Emmanuel de Martonne, Rodwell Jones, J. M. Wordie, H. J. Fleure and O. T. Jones amongst the lecturers in the spring session, all of them giving talks of high geographical content. Even the less famous speakers in between these great names dealt with geography rather than haphazard travels.

Barker went further still. He realized that members listening to the ordinary lectures were playing a very passive part in the Society and that good could be done by providing an opportunity for free discussion to a greater degree than could take place after the evening lectures. Those on the Council with long memories remembered with nostalgia those early "Library Meetings" in the Brown Street attics and the old Parsonage building. Thus was the Study Circle born again. Meeting fortnightly before the Tuesday evening meetings, it ran for most of the inter-war years, and under Barker's direction, brought not only members but also university students into highly interesting geographical discussions. To scan the list of speakers is to find mention of many names which have since become famous in the geographical world, and subjects which represent original research.

Thus in 1924 the Society presented a syllabus which can rarely, if ever, have been equalled. Most of the pre-war difficulties had vanished and the Council began to feel that after long tribulation the Society was about to forge ahead again.

With 1925 almost exactly the same pattern prevailed, and the new order became established custom. The Annual Meeting brought the retirement of D. A. Little as Hon. Treasurer and the appointment of F. B. Osborne, who, as F. B. Oppenheim, had been intimately connected with the Society for many years, and his father before him. Colonel Greg became Chairman of Council.

The previous November Harry Nuttall had died, and in 1925 the Society suffered the sad loss of Bishop Casartelli, that vigorous foundation member, and E. Pilkington, who had been one of the principal financial backers of the Building Company. As a result, a large number of shares came on the market, more than could be afforded. Loth to let the golden opportunity pass, seven members bought Life Subscriptions to enable as many as possible to be purchased.

Through diverting so much income to the purchase, the *Journal* had to suffer and it fell into arrears, instituting an economy which was to make its appearance more and more irregular until it finally ceased. On the other hand, over 4000 slides were presented by the executors of S. H. Brooks, and publishers generously supported the school textbook display so that it became a collection of real value. Moreover, the Building Company paid its first dividend for ten years.

The autumn activities of 1925 began with a visit from Captain Amundsen on 'My Polar Flight' and the list of lectures also included such names as F. Kingdon-Ward, but there were several signs that the general nature of the lectures was reverting towards, if not back to, the old level. A local society such as the Manchester Geographical Society must inevitably rely to a very large degree on lay support, and however much the trained geographers may champ at the bit, the interests of the majority who though untrained supply the bulk of the finances, must be studied.

Early in 1926 T. W. F. Parkinson died after eight years as an Honorary Secretary in which he led the struggle for better geographical education at advanced course level. Ever an active man, his death was directly attributed to overwork. To take his place, Council appointed L. M. Angus Butterworth.

Whilst lectures continued very much as before, the Council began to consider further steps to safeguard the position of geography at the university by means of an appeal for funds. The time, however, proved unpropitious for trade was wallowing in the depths of depression and there was also the General Strike. After conferences with the Vice-Chancellor, and the President of the Chamber of Commerce, Mellor and Crook, who were the leaders of the movement, agreed to leave the matter over.

Crook now reminded the Council that the next International Geographical Congress would be held in Cambridge in 1928, and out of the discussion of the part the Society could play in connection with this event, arose the suggestion that the publication of a volume of the *Journal* should be timed for the spring of that year, and that it should contain authoritative papers dealing with the North-west. As a result, several lectures on local topics found places in the 1927 lecture syllabus.

Colonel Crook's term as President came to an end in 1926, and as the desired successor could not be obtained, E. W. Mellor was persuaded to take office for a year. When a similar situation occurred a year later, Mellor insisted on resigning, and Colonel

74

Greg was elected to office, having served the Society in various capacities since 1901.

The first part of Greg's Presidency was uneventful, with the Society moving along in untroubled calm. The post-war renaissance had largely spent its force and activities had settled down again to their natural level. The only new development came in 1927 when summer excusions were resumed after a break of nearly twenty years. They became the responsibility of the Victorians, and the panel has continued to arrange them ever since. In the first few years visits were made to such places as Monsal Dale, the Ribble Valley, the Delamere Hills and Cresswell Crags, but even then antiquarian interests found their outlet in excursions to such buildings as Moreton Old Hall, Speke Hall, etc.

Towards the end of 1928 the Council made a determined attempt to increase the circulation of the *Journal*, basing their hopes on the success of the 1928 volume. The results were disappointing, being confined to a few reviews in the Press of various parts of Lancashire and Cheshire. Doubtless this might have been expected as the *Journal* had little appeal to the ordinary public.

About the same time the Council set up a committee with a view to coordinating geographical activity in the area, mainly in Manchester, but to include other towns. In April 1929 this committee approached the university with regard to establishing a Geographical Institute in the city which would coordinate the activities of the Study Circle, the Victorians, the Society's lectures, student activities and the local branches of the Geographical Association. Unfortunately Barker had fallen ill when the matter was ripe for discussion and without his energy and vision the project came to naught.

Meanwhile the educational watchdogs in the Society were awakened by a letter from H. W. Ogden, a prominent member, complaining that once again geography was falling into a sorry state in local secondary schools where pressure was being brought on children to give up the subject in favour of an extra language or a science subject for matriculation. The effect of such a policy prevented children from completing their basic course and also seriously reduced the number of Advanced Course candidates which would have an extremely bad influence on the future of geography. So unsatisfactory a position led to a special conference on 11 March 1929 at which a committee was set up to put things right again. The Council also arranged a *conversazione* to meet delegates attending a conference of students at the university.

Bad weather and prevalent epidemics greatly reduced the size of audiences during the spring of 1929 even though the programme included many outstanding speakers and attractive subjects. However, the worst misfortune occurred in June. For some months W. H. Barker had been ill, and on 19 June came the tragic news that he had died at the very early age of 46, whilst still in his prime and with many fruitful years ahead of him. Serious though the loss was to the Society members were still further distressed to find that he had died before being able to make satisfactory provision for his dependants. The warm tide of gratitude towards the man who had achieved so much in so short a time turned to practical help when, with the university, a special fund was set up to provide for the education of his son, and the Society collected more than half the total.

Within a short space followed the deaths of J. E. Balmer, an active member since 1888, and Professor T. F. Tout, a member since 1906. Serious though these losses of prominent personalities were, the Society was shortly to realize that they were but the first of many over the next four years which were to exercise a considerable change in its stature.

Though the lectures went on in much the same way during the winter 1929–30 and included such important visitors as Dr. (later Professor) L. D. Stamp and Professor G. Waterhouse, the Council had lost its fire. It seemed stunned by the loss of Barker, and did not even appoint a successor, so that the duties of Hon. Secretary were carried on by Angus Butterworth alone.

The spring of 1930 brought another heavy blow with the death of E. W. Mellor at the age of 77. He had been a member for thirty-nine years and had proved himself a pillar of strength not only as a counsellor and President, but as a lecturer and as a financial backer. Even after his death he became a benefactor, bequeathing the Society 54 more shares and bringing the total owned up to 480 out of the 555 issued. Fortunately, indeed, Sowerbutts was a Secretary of sterling worth, and he held the Society together through the troubled days, maintaining the lectures and getting the Study Circle to continue under the leadership of Walter Fitzgerald, then Lecturer in Geography at the university.

The summer posed a new problem as Greg's Presidency had come to an end and a successor had to be found. The choice fell on the fifth Lord Stanley of Alderley by virtue of his geographical interests, and happily he accepted.

Every cloud has its silver lining, and the university now reported that to succeed Barker they had appointed H. J. Fleure as Head of the Geography Department with the title of Professor. The fifty-year-long fight for the creation of a Chair of Geography at Manchester had been won, and the Society rejoiced, feeling no small satisfaction at the eminence and distinction of the man selected. Moreover, he was no stranger to the Society and in him they saw a worthy successor to Barker.

Fleure took up his appointment in October 1930. With him from Aberystwyth he brought the Headquarters of the Geographical Association, and its Library was set up in the Manchester High School of Commerce where it was to remain for some twenty years. The Society's finances would not allow them to take over additional floor-space in the Parsonage to accommodate the books there, but at least Manchester had another claim in the geographical world.

The silver lining, however, was only to be glimpsed through a rift in the clouds, and the winter of 1930–31 brought back gloomy days. Membership was steadily dropping, and the adverse effect this had on income compelled the Council to restrict the size of the *Journal*. They were loth for it to be discontinued, however, and so they invited Fitzgerald to take over the Editorship with a view to producing something, however small. Fitzgerald declined the invitation, pleading that he could not spare the time as he had additional teaching responsibilities at Liverpool University in connection with Roxby's absence in China. Thus the *Journal* lapsed, and many thought its resumption unlikely.

Realizing that the condition of the Society had greatly deteriorated since the great days of 1923–24, the Council invited Fleure to fill Barker's position as Hon. Secretary but in this, too, the Department could not help the Society, Fleure pleading that for the moment he needed to devote all his energies to his new Department.

The officers and Sowerbutts managed to provide an attractive syllabus with the customary occasional distinguished speaker, but with an increasing number of members lecturing as the financial position deteriorated. Nevertheless, a feeling of fatalism spread amongst the members, and the growing despondency found expression in the fact that only sixty-six people attended the Annual Dinner in November.

To make matters worse, the President, Lord Stanley of Alderley, died whilst still in office. A new choice was made but the candidate declined. The position had now become serious and the Council saw that if the Society were to survive it must have a strong lead from somebody who not only believed in it wholeheartedly but also enjoyed the confidence of the members. Accordingly they asked Colonel Greg to serve a second period of office, and he, well understanding what was at stake, consented. All these difficulties and attendant negotiations had, however, caused delays and as a result the Annual Meeting did not take place until October.

To maintain the regular weekly meetings in the face of dwindling funds, the Council had to rely, once again, on the members themselves during the winter 1931–32. Fortunately there were men such as T. A. Edwards, Charles Eastwood, and Charles Sutton who had travelled extensively, whilst Professor Fleure contributed his share. With this support, and a few outside speakers, including Sir Arnold Wilson in connection with the Annual Dinner, the programme could be presented in full.

The spring of 1932 brought the crux of the situation. The general world economic position had not improved to any marked extent and the Society's finances were at such a low ebb that Sowerbutts voluntarily gave up part of his already meagre salary to relieve the strain. Moreover, with the deaths of Theodore Gregory, a foundation member and Auditor until 1914, S. L. Keymer, a Trustee for over forty years, and Albert Wilmore, the Council had lost still more of its elder statesmen.

When Greg realized that his second Presidency would be for a full term of three years and not just for a stopgap period, he began more actively to stimulate the flagging interest of members. His first step was to arrange for the Annual Meeting to be held at his lovely home in the Bollin Valley: Norcliffe Hall, Styal. This had the desired effect and the attendance there was greater than for some years. Then a Finance Committee consisting of Crook,

Ginger, Whitby and the Secretary received instructions to find ways and means of overcoming the deficit. This led to the establishment of the 'Crowns' Appeal Fund, and members responded so well, even gratefully, to this positive lead that by the end of 1932 over £160 had been collected, and the Society could repay its debt of honour to the Secretary.

Whilst the appeal gradually acquired momentum, special attention went into the preparation of the autumn programme in order to revive membership. The speakers included Bertram Thomas, Professor Roxby (now back from China) and Sir William Himbury, whilst Dr. H. R. Mill spoke on his favourite 'Antarctic Research' during a visit which included a highly successful Annual Dinner.

Encouraged by the favourable trend of events, and the new hope that was dawning, Council decided that, to further encourage new members, subscriptions should run from the first of any month instead, as hitherto, only from 1st January. Thus, by the end of 1932 the worst of the storm had been weathered even if the Society remained weaker than many thought desirable. However, the Study Circle had ceased by Christmas 1932.

Meanwhile, the workers of the Society had not been idle, but had laboured steadily in its cause even to the extent of giving practical as well as moral support to the Liverpool Geographical Society which had fared even worse than its Manchester counterpart. Besides the lectures, the Victorians gave an average of about another thirty each year, and also lent their help to the Lord Mayor's Unemployment Scheme. Then, when some of his former students opened a fund to provide a Barker prize in geography at the university, the Council donated the £36 balance left in the Chair of Geography account for this purpose.

As the spring of 1933 gradually unfolded, the Crowns Appeal reached £300 and enabled the Council to pay all its debts. Yet, just when complete recovery seemed within its grasp, there came another severe blow: the death in December 1933 of T. W. Sowerbutts, that charming personality, loyal servant and painstaking official who had acted as Secretary ever since 1919 and had thus helped to guide the Society through the difficult post-war period and the anxious years of the Depression.

The Council had no particular successor in mind, and, in the circumstances, it was decided to appoint the Librarian, Arthur Marshman, for the time being. Marshman had been with the Society since 1899 and had an intimate knowledge of its ways, and he was devoted to the study of geography. In the event, he proved himself well able to discharge the duties of Secretary with the backing of the Executive Committee. Though the appointment was never confirmed, he continued in this office until his retirement in April 1956, at the age of 70, his helpful manner and kindly ways becoming an integral and traditional feature of the Society's life. In 1933 Professor Fleure was appointed as an Hon. Secretary to fill the vacancy left by Barker's death in 1929.

Encouraged by the recovery of the Society Greg again invited members to Norcliffe Hall for the Annual Meeting. Liverpool, however, lacked the resistance apparent in Manchester, and the strain proved too great for its Geographical Society which went into liquidation in June 1933.

The Arthur Marshman Era
1933–50

Though the syllabus for the winter 1933–34 still contained the names of many members, after Christmas conditions enabled more visitors to be brought in: such people for example as F. Spencer Chapman, who at that time was much concerned with the Arctic. The Society also embarked on a public lecture at which Frank Smythe described the latest attempt to climb Mount Everest.

As spring gave way to summer, the Council began to consider what should be done to celebrate the Jubilee which fell in October. They could not undertake anything lavish as they were still beset with money troubles, but they were equally determined that some appropriate celebration should be held.

Professor Fleure headed a group which claimed that the most practical step would be to resume publication of the *Journal*. For nearly ten years it had been in abeyance, and without a *Journal*, a Society lost caste. He carried the day, and H. W. Ogden was asked to take over the editing. Owing to pressure of other work, he had to decline, and the Hon. Editorship then passed into the hands of Mrs. Mabel Wright, then in the university's Department of Geography. Her terms of reference were to produce a regular magazine containing contributions of real value to geographical science. This she did, and the resumed *Journal* began to show promise, even though it never attained the excellence of the earlier issues.

Other arrangements had begun to take shape when, in September, Colonel Greg died suddenly. There was little time to grieve so sad a loss for urgent action must be taken. Accordingly a deputation set out for Alderley to ask the 6th Lord Stanley to accept nomination. The latter rose to the occasion splendidly, and the situation was saved; the Jubilee celebrations could go forward.

The autumn lectures, which brought many outstanding speakers, began with an introductory talk about the Society's activities from 1884 to 1934 by George Ginger, an active and constructively useful member of the Council since 1907. Unfortunately the material on which his remarks were based cannot be traced. The Jubilee itself was marked by a lecture on "Persia" by Percy Sykes on 18 October, and the next day followed a Jubilee Dinner at the Queen's Hotel with Major General Sir Percy Cox as principal guest. Lord Stanley, the new President, showed that he had soon made himself at home in his new office, and the attendance and general success of the function silenced even the severest critics.

With a view to maintaining the new enthusiasm, the Council held a referendum on the most popular time for holding the evening meetings, in which the majority voted for retaining the traditional 7.30 p.m. At the same time, Machin, J. W. Price and Matthew Grainger formed a Committee to keep the Society before the public. They seem to have considered numerous plans, but without achieving anything positive.

About this time, the Society also lost Colonel Crook, J. W. Robson and C. H. Bellamy, all of them with considerable periods of service on the Council to their credit. With their passing, nearly all the threads with the past had been lost. The first half of the 1930s had indeed seen the departure of the stalwarts, and their replacement by members of a new generation. Curiously, this change of personnel—no less than fifteen new names were added to the Council in 1930 to 1935—coincided with the beginning of a new phase in the Society's activities although the effect was not to be seen for several years yet. Born of adversity, nurtured with militant missionary zeal, it had, with the creation of the Chair of Geography, achieved one of its main objectives, and the subject was now in a far better state than in 1884. A spirit of complacency began to creep into the Council, and its members were content to let the Society's activities reduce themselves to lectures and outings.

Fortunately, the lectures maintained a high standard, and if there was a tendency to include much that could be described as travel, and little that could be called geography, the Council at least had the sound defence that local geographers gave the Society such poor support that programmes had to be arranged to attract lay members if it was to continue. It was in other spheres of activity, however, where the Council failed to take interest.

For a time Fleure and Mrs Wright brought the academic view before the Council, but in 1935 the former found his commitments in other directions so great, and the inertia of the Council so marked, that he resigned from his Hon. Secretaryship. To take his place, the Council elected Henry Forsyth, who though having served an apprenticeship of only one year on the Council, had revealed his sympathies with the work of the Society and the charm and ability to further it.

During 1935, more visiting lecturers were used, and the Society organized more public lectures, the first by Colonel Stewart Blacker on his flight over Everest, the second by H. W. Tilman on the Himalayas, the third by Martin Lindsay on 'Crossing the Greenland Ice Cap'.

Mrs. Wright raised the question of the Study Circle in the autumn, and put in a plea for its resumption. As a result Matthew Grainger volunteered to act as Leader and meetings began again in the spring of 1936. The circle met at approximately fortnightly intervals, and immediately before the Tuesday evening lectures. As before, a proportion of speakers was drawn from senior students and research assistants at the university, which ensured a fairly advanced level of interest and an excellent opportunity for the exchange of views. The discussions were often quite lively and members were loth to terminate the meetings at 7.30 when the main lectures began.

The Victorians continued relatively active, though they found that the demand for their services had decreased in face of the growing popularity of the 'talkies' and of the wireless. Nevertheless, the group delivered 33 talks in 1935 and 44 in 1936 to some of the many clubs and organizations in the district. They also arranged annual programmes of three or four excursions to places of interest. For example, in 1935 there were trips to Ingleton, the Yorkshire Moors and to the Dove and Manifold Valleys.

In other ways too, the Society consolidated its recovery. The Annual Dinners became an established feature with encouraging attendances. In 1935, Sir Josiah Stamp came as chief guest, and Sir Edward Grigg the following year. The collection too received continual additions, specially notable being a valuable map collection from the late Colonel Crook, and numerous lantern slides and African ethnological specimens from Colonel Ainsworth.

In 1936 Lord Stanley of Alderley resigned from the Presidency, and at the Annual Meeting, held at Chinley, F. B. Osborne, a member of the Council since 1907 and Hon. Treasurer since 1925, was elected to succeed him. Once again the direction of the Society had passed into the care of a working member who brought to his office the clear head of a lawyer.

The same meeting saw a change of Editor. A large group in the Council strenuously voiced their opinion that the contents of the *Journal* had become too academic, and held little interest 'for the ordinary members'. The new generation of lay councillors were beginning to make their presence felt. During the next fifteen years, this group was to achieve considerable success, and to imperil the worth of the body which they governed. Certainly they nullified any influence which the Society exercised in the geographical world, and they left it little more than a travel club. Mrs. Wright adopted the only course open to her and resigned. Pending new arrangements, L. M. Angus Butterworth, one of the Hon. Secretaries, took over the *Journal*, but even then his hands were tied by the setting up of an Editorial Committee 'to assist in the preparation of papers for publication'.

Though men like Osborne, Forsyth, Royce and Grainger still had a voice on the Council, the 'new generation' seemed to carry the day, and for the next years complacency and self-satisfaction were the keynotes. The effect on the *Journal* is evident, but more insidious was the lack of staff. The temporary appointment of Arthur Marshman on the death of T. W. Sowerbutts meant that the staff had been reduced to the Secretary alone. In the financial crisis that followed, this taxed the Society's resources to the full, but when conditions improved it was allowed to become the established practice. Membership showed little prospect of increasing so that there was never much money for appointing additional staff, and the Council were reluctant to raise the subscriptions lest more members should resign. Nevertheless, the problem remained that the amount of work needed to maintain the Society in a sound condition was more than one man could accomplish. Arthur Marshman made a brave attempt to cope with the situation, but inevitably ordinary routine work fell into arrears. Here indeed was the great opportunity for the Victorians, the worker-geographers, to come to the rescue, but they were found wanting, they had degenerated into nothing more than an association of travel lecturers.

Fleure and the staff of his department would have given assistance even under such adverse conditions, had an appeal been made to them, but the 'new generation', acutely aware of their geographical shortcomings, and fearful of their own eclipse, would have as little connection as possible with the university, and a curious antagonism grew up which persisted until several years after the 1939–45 war. Thus Osborne's Presidency was an unhappy period when, considering the excellence of the man, one might have reasonably expected great advances.

This same year brought the sad death of George V who had been so long connected with the Society as President, and on ascending the throne, as Patron, Edward VIII graciously consented to become Patron in his father's stead, and when George VI succeeded his brother, the Patronage was again continued.

The abilities of the few kept the Society alive over the next few years, and though the number of members contributing papers on 'The Romance of Ruritania' tended to increase, there was a leavening of better-quality material. The desire for this better type of geographical information is witnessed by the healthy state of the Study Circle, which with an enthusiastic group of about thirty at its meetings, heard papers containing first-class information. From Matthew Grainger, the leadership passed to Thomas Warburton in 1937.

At the suggestion of W. H. Zimmern, a 'Corporate membership' was developed whereby commercial and industrial firms, hospitals, etc., could join the Society for two guineas per annum, receiving two transferable tickets for all the Society's activities. In the next few years, many organizations took advantage of this new facility, but it has never achieved the popularity that one might have expected in a city such as Manchester.

As tension mounted in Europe, the Society peacefully followed its customary way to the autumn. H. W. Tilman gave two public lectures on 'Everest 1937' and Admiral Sir William Goodenough attended the Annual Dinner.

Early in 1939, the Society had the rare pleasure of hearing one of its own members, Norman Pye, lecture on original research which he had carried out the previous summer in Spitzbergen. Only in April did a lecture on Czechoslovakia by E. H. Madden reveal any awareness of events inside Europe.

In the summer of 1939, the termination of Osborne's maximum

period of office raised the difficult question of a worthy successor. After considering several possible candidates, the Presidency was offered to Sir Henry Fildes, a leading industrialist, and an experienced member of Parliament who had been a Vice-President for some eleven years. Though an extremely busy man, he accepted and was duly elected at an Annual Meeting held at the Palace Hotel, Buxton (Greg's innovation had been continued through the years, and the Annual Meeting was now held in connection with an excursion). In this case Sir Henry later invited members to his home and gardens at Kerridge, near Bollington. This choice of candidate was extremely popular, for Sir Henry had the reputation of being as warm-hearted as he was industrious, and members felt the solution ideal considering that the possible field had lately been narrowed by the untimely deaths of Bardsley, Gamble and Ginger, three senior members of proved enthusiasm and ability, who must otherwise have been strong contenders for office.

Owing to business reasons, Angus Butterworth resigned from the Hon. Secretaryship he had held for thirteen difficult years, being succeeded by Major William Cross, a Councillor of long standing and one of the Trustees. Angus Butterworth however agreed to continue editing the *Journal* for the time being.

Before Sir Henry Fildes could preside at his first meeting, the second world war had been unleashed. The local authorities were advisedly alarmed at the threatened effects of air raids, and the Council was well aware of the difficulties arising from the 'black out' and transport problems. The outcome was the suspension of all lectures. Members fully realized the wisdom of such a step in the circumstances, but as time passed and the anticipated horrors failed to materialize, more and more began to ask that some effort should be made to resume them, even if the programme had to be modified or curtailed. The Council welcomed such a lead because the cessation of lectures for an indefinite period would gravely harm the Society if it did not bring it to an end. To find out how many members would attend resumed lectures, the Council held a postal ballet, and of those replies received, 36 per cent favoured continuing. Thus encouraged, it was decided to begin lectures again from January 1940, starting at 6.30 instead of 7.30.

With the war, lecturers could only be obtained with the greatest difficulty, but members came to the rescue, and the spring programme of nine lectures provided a distinguished list, and included Professor Fleure and John Coatman. In co-operation with the 'Friends of Czechoslovakia' the Society was privileged to entertain Jan Masaryk who spoke on his ravished homeland. The Study Circle however had to be abandoned, but the Victorian lectures came to be in great demand, and with the summer excursions were resumed. The first shock of war had been withstood, and by adjusting itself to the new conditions the Society could continue; indeed it had a useful role to play. However, the Executive Committee ceased to function at the end of 1939 due to curtailment of activity.

With the fall of France in 1940, the war entered a new and more hostile phase which was brought home to the Society with the Christmas raids on the city. The building itself suffered damage from both incendiary bombs and blast, but fortunately not sufficient to make it unusable. The attacks, however, acted as a warning, and lecture times were altered. Until the Normandy invasion in 1944, lectures began only in February going on into May, and then from September until November. On the darker winter evenings they started as early as 6 p.m. and in February and November they were given at 2.30 on Saturdays.

The Manchester Microscopical Society fared less well, being bombed out of their quarters and so they were offered hospitality which they gladly accepted. Similarly, the Literary and Philosophical Society were offered the use of the Geographical Hall. With the renewal of activity, and with the Victorians again delivering over a hundred lectures a year—many of them at the request of the Committee for Education in H.M. Forces—Henry Forsyth decided that the time had come for him to retire from the Hon. Secretaryship to make way for somebody younger. The choice fell on Miss Ethel Pickering, a relatively new member who had been appointed to the Council only the previous year. A retired Post Office Official, she had travelled widely and spent a long period in East Africa, and she had given many lectures in all parts of the country. Most important of all, though, she had the interest and the time for the job. She took up her duties in June 1941.

Miss Pickering had no enviable task. Wartime conditions were difficult enough in themselves, but in addition to finding lecturers and helping an overworked Marshman with the Victorian lectures, she had to reconcile the 'new generation' and the 'geographers' on the Council, to do her best to maintain membership and generally to see that the Society emerged from the war in a fit state to continue. That she succeeded is now evident, and her success may be attributed to her geniality, her sense of balance and also to the fact that her sex gave her a certain advantage.

For the next few years, the general pattern of the Society's activities remained much the same, with some twenty-four evening lectures and four or five excursions each year. As travel restrictions grew stricter, the excursions came to be more and more local, but this was met by taking the opportunity to visit local works and factories, and for trips such as that to study the geology of Alderley Edge under the leadership of Dr. Jackson of Manchester Museum.

The *Journal* fared badly, especially with restrictions on the supply of paper. The standard fell sharply with the volume for 1940–41 and only recovered slightly with that for 1942–44.

In 1942 Major William Cross's long service to the Society brought him to the Presidency in succession to Sir Henry Fildes, and his post as second Hon. Secretary was never filled, so that from this time onward the main work of the Society fell on to the shoulders of Marshman and Miss Pickering. At this same meeting, W. H. Zimmern became Chairman of Council.

In the autumn, and in spite of the 'black out', attendances at lectures gradually increased from an average of 57 to 68, helped by their being thrown open to members of the Forces. The Victorians too found themselves busier than ever, collaborating extensively with the W.E.A., the Lancashire and Cheshire Economic League, youth organizations, etc. Their slide resources were greatly improved by the gift of nearly nine hundred views of East Africa from Alderman T. A. Edwards, whilst Warburton made possible the purchase of another large collection covering all the world. Increasingly severe restrictions on travel, however, seriously curtailed the excursions, limiting them to places of interest within or near the city.

Though a reasonable programme of lectures could be provided, 1943 was undoubtedly the time during which the effects of the war were most keenly felt. But as 1944 came, so too did the feeling that it had passed its crux. This in turn gave place to a quiet optimism. Though the lectures still avoided the dark nights of

December and January, more and more people began to attend until audiences of a hundred, even a hundred and fifty could be recorded.

Apart from the war itself, changes were inevitable. In January 1944, with the death of F. B. Osborne, the Society lost one of its stalwarts. Then shortly afterwards Charles Sutton died after an active membership since 1912, particularly as a popular Victorian lecturer. Finally, in September, Fleure had to retire from his Chair at the university after reaching the age limit. His place was taken by Walter Fitzgerald, a member of the Society.

Returning confidence found its expression in the autumn of 1944, when on 14 October the Diamond Jubilee of the foundation was celebrated by a luncheon at the Reform Club attended by over 150 members and guests. Apart from the satisfaction of knowing that the Society had endured the worst days of the war, those present felt that its struggles for geographical education had not been in vain when the newly elected Professor Fitzgerald stated that his Department was almost embarrassed by the great number of students who wished to take the subject, and that he was finding it necessary to turn away applicants from all parts of the country.

The spectacular collapse of Germany made it abundantly clear that peace would not be long delayed, and thoughts turned towards what should be done when it returned. In January 1945, Fitzgerald gave a lead with a talk on 'What Geography Means to Me' in which he reviewed the effect of two wars on geographical development and suggested what its future course should be. There was talk also of reviving the Study Circle, but the Council, after six or seven years of inertia, lacked members with sufficient drive to achieve any positive development.

In February 1945 R. S. Booth reminded the Council that, for many years before the war, a special Christmas lecture had been held for the children of members and their friends. Such occasions had always been extremely popular, and he now suggested that this activity should be widened in scope and that the Society should present geographical lectures to local school children. The idea received a warm welcome, and a special committee of Booth, Fitzgerald, Price and the Misses Pickering and Roper worked out the practical details. They then approached W. T. Stevenson,

Chief Inspector of Schools for the Manchester Education Committee who strongly supported the project, and so the series began and has ever since continued with the help of the Education Committee. The lectures achieved instant success, with over 700 applications for the first 300 seats, and each of the four lectures that winter were over-subscribed. Such enthusiasm became evident in fact that a new category of membership (Junior Student) was established for pupils under 19 years of age.

The Annual Meeting of 1945 brought to the Presidency W. H. Zimmern, thus emphasizing a proud family association, for his grandfather had been the Society's first Chairman, his father the first Hon. Secretary, and other relations too had held office. He himself had been intimately connected with the Society all his days, and latterly he had built up for himself a reputation for wisdom in its deliberations. At this juncture, no better man could have taken over the presidential responsibilities.

Another change at this time was the resignation of L. M. Angus Butterworth from the Editorship owing to pressure of business. With the war, his period of office had been beset with many difficulties, and he never had the opportunity to produce the standard of *Journal* he desired. With the ending of hostilities, a better and a regular magazine had become of prime importance, and he preferred to hand over to a successor with more time to devote to it.

Edwin Royce had capabilities which promised well for the future, but tragically he died before the end of the year and before he could take up his task.

Though the actual fighting had ceased, the world had by no means recovered, but it became a little easier to obtain outside speakers, and names such as Lord Rennell of Rodd and Professor Fawcett began to appear on the programmes again. Released from destructive efforts, Man turned towards re-construction, with re-planning and re-building a new world subjects on every lip, and the Society reacted to this by organizing a short series of lectures on Manchester before and after the war which led, in the autumn of 1946, to others on aspects of housing. This more practical approach can be attributed largely to the initiative of T. L. Green, a former Inspector of Schools and now on the staff of the university's Department of Education. About this time he gave great help to Miss Pickering in the preparation of the syllabus, being perhaps the first representative of a younger generation who realized that the Society had, over the last fifteen or twenty years, allowed its old standards to fall, and that if it were to regain its former influence, it must concern itself more with geography and less with travel. This began a struggle between the younger, more progressive elements with the Society and the older conservative members who, with no geographical training, no militant geographical philosophy, were content to drift along.

Progress, if slow, was nevertheless real, and good groundwork and the support of voluntary workers such as Captain H. P. Beatty, led the following year to an increased membership and to larger audiences. The calls on the Victorians, however, declined, only about sixteen lectures being delivered by the panel. The return to normality also permitted a more ambitious programme of summer outings to which members reacted with enthusiasm. To the visits to industrial concerns, collieries, river boards, etc., it became possible to add longer trips to houses and other places of architectural and archaeological interest. Probably because many of those responsible for drawing up the programmes had these archaeological interests, and few if any had geographical abilities, the geographical content of these outings fell very low and, even then, the leaders failed to use the opportunities that offered themselves. On the other hand, they provided members with a chance to get to know each other better, thus encouraging the social side of the Society's activities.

Very unfortunately business reasons compelled Zimmern to resign from the Presidency before the end of the customary three-year period, and he made way for the election of Alderman T. A. Edwards, another cotton merchant and one who had travelled widely in East and South Africa. With his long knowledge of the Society (dating from the time when he had carried some slave chains to the Free Trade Hall for one of Stanley's lectures) and his knowledge of the Manchester business world, he will be remembered chiefly for his energetic campaign to interest local firms in the advantages of Corporate Membership.

At the Annual Meeting in Salford Town Hall, Norman Pye, then Lecturer in Geography at the university, and another of the progressive elements in the Society, delivered a thoughtful address on 'The Nature of Geography and the Role of the Local Society' in which he endeavoured to point the direction of future developments and to avert the threatened deterioration into a travel club.

The official response to this appeal proved very disappointing, but his remarks encouraged a few members to ask for more geographical topics and less travel talks amongst the lectures. Miss Pickering responded to the urgings of this group by inviting such lecturers as Wing Commander D. C. McKinley on the 'R.A.F. North Polar Investigation Flights', Brigadier Bagnold on 'Desert Sand Dunes', Leonard Brooks on 'Geography in Education and Citizenship' and J. M. Wordie on the 'Falkland Islands Dependencies'. At the same time, she found herself hampered by the need to maintain membership (and of course finance) by catering for the non-technical tastes of the majority. Though she well understood the pleas of the progressives, she could point out that the Society was kept alive by its rank and file, whereas the younger generation and the trained geographers were few in number, support from the university in particular being very disappointing.

Whilst this dichotomy continued beneath the surface, the audiences at evening lectures steadily grew larger, and it became apparent that the Society had weathered the storms of the last decade. Alderman Edwards set a good example by attending every lecture except when out of Manchester representing the Society. He had its cause very near to his heart, and when he found that the popularity of the Children's Lectures had further increased, he opened negotiations with the Manchester Education Committee which led, in 1948, to that body making the Society a grant in aid, support which has continued and increased and is appreciated not only for its very real financial assistance, but also for its moral encouragement.

Unable to make significant progress in the lecture field, the rebel element turned their attentions to the Library which had been steadily growing over the years and was now very full. The need for maintaining the income from other tenants of the building precluded the Society from taking over more floor space, as had been envisaged in 1905. Instead, useless books were weeded out and the remainder rearranged on a regional basis—hitherto books had been added in order of acquisition which made finding them extremely difficult, particularly as the classification of new additions was not always up to date.

The Society's general policy in 1949 continued that of the two previous years, with the occasional more technical lecture sandwiched between travelogues. To the delight of the progressives, some of the more difficult subjects like 'The Exploration of the Oceans' by Professor W. J. Pugh aroused great enthusiasm amongst the ordinary members, suggesting that the conservatism of the Council rather than that of the Society was at fault. On the other hand, the interest of the public at large in geography, as indicated by the call on the Victorians, fell to its lowest figure since the panel was created.

The most interesting domestic event of 1949 took place at the beginning of October when the Society publicly expressed its appreciation of Arthur Marshman who the previous June had completed fifty years' service, first as office boy, then as Librarian and since 1933 as Secretary. During the course of the opening meeting, a presentation was made, and nine or ten members paid tribute to his unfailing loyalty, his helpfulness towards all those who sought his help, his resourcefulness and his modesty. In his reply, Marshman recalled events of moment in the history of the Society, recollections that stretched back to the days of Eli Sowerbutts. Though the pilot version of this history was written in his lifetime and though he took it home to read and enlarge, his health had then begun to give way, and so a great store of knowledge has been lost.

With the repetition in 1949–50 of the previous pattern of activities, it became clear that it now represented the permanent pattern, one which differed in several respects from that of the pre-war years. In the new conditions, active members were preponderantly female, and in the age distribution the younger generations are poorly represented. The administration too consisted mainly of the older members who had supported the Society through the war years, a position made worse by the fact that whereas the President must resign after three years, Councillors were appointed *sine die* so that new blood could only be introduced when a vacancy occurred through death or rare resignation, giving the ordinary members little encouragement to interest themselves in the welfare of the Society.

Since the departure of Professor Fleure, the Society and the university Department of Geography had lost touch with each other. Professor Fitzgerald never had a very close association with the Society and his tenure of the Chair of Geography was cut short by his premature death.

At the Annual Meeting in 1950, Alderman Edwards completed the maximum tenure of office, and Mr. R. S. Booth succeeded him as President. The latter had been an active member for many years, latterly as Chairman of Council, and had, as recorded, founded the Children's Lectures. At the same meeting, Major Cross handed over the Hon. Editorship to T. N. L. Brown.

Index